Kernel Lessons *Plus*

A post-intermediate course
Students' Book

ROBERT O'NEILL

Eurocentre   Longman

Foreword

Acknowledgements

The first four publications from the Eurocentres were intended solely for the teacher. The fifth, *English in Situations*, was course material for the use of both teacher and student.

Kernel Lessons Intermediate was a new development in that it contained a full programme of material specially designed for the student. We believe that with *Kernel Lessons Plus* we are continuing to meet a real need, and that teachers and students at this particular level will find more interest, satisfaction and challenge in both language teaching and learning.

The accompanying Teacher's Book gives a full description of how this material can be put to the best use. Both the techniques recommended and the material itself are based on long experience of English language teaching gained at the English Eurocentres. Whereas the use of language is somewhat controlled initially, the final objective of this book is that the student should be able to express his ideas fluently in his own manner.

Erh. J. C. Waespi
Director of the Foundation for
European Language and
Educational Centres.

The Eurocentres are a group of language schools directed by the Foundation for European Language and Educational Centres, Zürich. The schools offer full-time courses for adult students all the year round, and each language is taught in the country where it is spoken.

Many many people deserve thanks for help given while this book was being written. I can mention only a few of the many. They are:

Mr R. H. Kingsbury, who was concerned with the initial planning stages of the whole course, and contributed significantly to the Tests and Teacher's Book.

Mr Erh. J. C. Waespi, Director of the Foundation for European Language and Educational Centres, without whose support and encouragement the book could never have been written at all.

The staffs of the London and Bournemouth Eurocentres who, as before, contributed a mass of very useful comment, criticism and suggestions.

Miss P. Charles, who typed and re-typed the original manuscript in its various drafts and did much of the collation for the book.

Robert O'Neill
October, 1972.

Contents

UNIT 5
The rich and the poor

UNIT 6
Holidays

UNIT 7
Disaster

UNIT 8
Letters to an advice column

UNIT 13
Women's Liberation

Lesson 25 *(page 104)*

Wish + would, were, etc.
    I wish my wife would stay at home.
    I wish I earned a bit more money.
    Some women wish they had been born men.

Lesson 26 *(page 108)*

She decided she would rather take a train than go by car.
She wondered if there was any point in waiting.
I think I'd rather . . . than . . .
What's the use of just looking at it?
Phrasal verbs with two particles
    He put up with it.

UNIT 14
Inflation

Lesson 27 *(page 112)*

Verbs like *give*, with direct and indirect objects
Verbs like *explain*, with direct and indirect objects
Passive forms of verbs like *give, explain*
I can't afford to have it done.
I've just had it done.

Lesson 28 *(page 116)*

She left, saying she would be back later.
She told him not to do it.
How much should it cost to have it done?
Omission of *have* after *want, would like*, etc
    I want the engine looked at.
Inseparable phrasal verbs
    I'll see to it.

UNIT 15
Progress

Lesson 29 *(page 120)*

Zero article
    We have made progress in industry, science and medicine.
Modification of nouns with and without zero article
    Modern industry
    The car industry

Lesson 30 *(page 124)*

She had been one of the last to come.
She waited for the blow to come.
I was going to do it but I forgot.
I'd like to have avoided it.
Intransitive phrasal verbs
    The fire broke out.

To the student

Kernel Lessons Plus is designed for students who have acquired a basic knowledge mastery of the patterns and structures in books such as *Kernel Lessons Intermediate*. This book will build upon this foundation, revise it, and further extend it.

Kernel Lessons Plus is designed to do these things.

(a) It will give you a chance to look again at some of the most important things in English, but you will learn *new uses* of these things here.

(b) It will introduce you to a great number of completely new patterns, forms and structures.

(c) It will introduce you to many of the ideas and themes that people all over the world are talking about in the 1970s, and will still be talking about in the 1980s. But, just as important, it will introduce you to the language you will need to talk about these things yourself.

(d) It will introduce you to a wide variety of everyday situations and conversations.

(e) It will give you a chance to listen to tape recordings of English people speaking naturally and at normal speed. There are special pages throughout the book that give you the meaning of some of the words they use, and ask you questions about what they say.

(f) It will give you a chance to use English to say *what you want to say* and not just what is in the book. There are a large number of special questions for discussion and also a large number of special exercises (called "transfer exercises") that make you think of your own examples of what you have learned and make you use these examples in everyday situations.

To make use of *Kernel Lessons Plus* please note the following things.

(a) The book has fifteen units
(b) Each unit is divided into two lessons. In other words there are thirty lessons in all.
(c) Each unit is about a particular theme, such as "Crime and Punishment", "Inflation", etc.
(d) Each unit has the following parts:

1 Texts and Pictures

These are very short texts about the "theme" of each unit. You must do far more than simply read and understand these texts. *You* must often ask questions, answer questions, and use the language of the texts to discuss the ideas in them.

2 Grammar exposition and exercises

This consists of two pages of comment and exercises. The comment is very short and not too technical. The exercises will help you to find out if you *can use* what you have learned in a variety of new situations.

3 Intensive listening

This is the page in each unit that goes with the tape recording of people speaking quickly and naturally.

4 Short story excerpt

This is a short text. Each text is about three radio reporters and their secretary, and the problems they have. There are special vocabulary and other exercises.

5 Dialogue

This is always a short conversation. It is always based on the short story excerpt you have just read. There is a tape recording of each conversation. You must listen to it, or to the teacher reading it. On this page one part of the conversation is always missing. This is the part you must listen to very carefully and later play yourself. You will learn a lot of everyday language, useful phrases and patterns when you do this.

6 Summary and revision

This is always the last page of the unit. It explains small points, does special revision and gives you homework.

1

Traffic in our cities

1

This is a traffic jam. Most of these people are trying to get to work. They all work in the city but few of them live there. They are feeling very angry and frustrated at the moment because the traffic is hardly moving. Traffic jams like this happen every day. The problem is getting worse all the time.

Paired Practice

Imagine you are a reporter. You are interviewing some of the drivers in this traffic jam. What questions do you ask? Give the answers as well! You want to know:

1 where they are going
2 where they work
3 where they live
4 how they are feeling at the moment
5 why
6 how often these jams happen
7 if things are getting better

2

This policeman is directing traffic in the centre of London. He does this every day. He often suffers from headaches. He simply does not get enough oxygen.

Questions

Ask the policeman:
1 what he is doing
2 if he does this every day
3 why he suffers from headaches
Give the answers as well.

3

Professor Colin Campbell is a famous traffic expert. He believes that most of our cities are dying. "Most of our cities are being destroyed by the motor car," he is saying. At the moment he is being interviewed on television.

Questions

a
1 Who is this man?
2 What does he believe?
3 What is happening at the moment?

b
Now interview him yourself. Ask:
1 what is happening to our cities
2 what they are being destroyed by

Mother says "It's a scandal!"

Craven Road looks like a thousand other roads. But Mrs. Nora Clay describes it as "a scandal and a death trap". She is organising a protest march.

Her eight year old son, Donald, walks along Craven Road every day and crosses it on his way to school. More than 100 other schoolchildren do the same thing. The road is also used by heavy lorries and other motor traffic all day long. Yesterday Donald was knocked down by a lorry and almost killed.

"The road's far too dangerous for children to cross alone," his mother said. "There aren't even any traffic lights there! The authorities know how dangerous it is but they never do anything about it! Two other children were knocked down at the same place last month. One of them was almost killed."

Mrs. Clay's son is still in hospital. "He's suffering from shock but luckily no bones were broken," a doctor said.

(partial left column, torn:)

blew in the
10 shops in
Street, off
.don, yester-
e were hurt.
e shows the

gas main
and police
uated the
ice official
.nto a num-
make sure
own inside.
y an Act of
this if it's
y in the
."

using a
tes form-
the new
ine when
.d caught

: "There
.tes in the
.cked pipe
trying to
fire and
.as I was
.ole."

(partial centre column, torn:)

.f motorway bo:
with links to
network. This
major recomm
the Layfield in
Greater Lond
ment Plan, wh
published this

Mr Geoffrey Ri
for the Envir
the same time
statement to
in a form which
leave maxim
manoeuvre. '7
larly crucial
GLC election
when the Cc
be hard pr
control.

The Labour F
stated firml
build the
ring and w.
cash in on
motorway o
Government's
back only one
near the cen'
Labour, if it
opposition a,
cept, without.
plans at all.

Both the Labou
tive groups
believe in t
outer ring
called Ring

Orbit

However, the
suggests tha
necessary in
ernment's
orbital rou
only a few
This makes
Three to th
but it woul
that extent.

Indeed, the G
object to
for more th
the grounds
council estat
and lack of
consultation.

The Layfield,
its first pub
summer of
virtually ev
don life, in
housing,
chairman
field, a
QC, w
fc

4

This newspaper article presents another aspect of the traffic problem.

Questions

You are interviewing Mrs Clay.
Ask her:

1 how old her son is
2 how often he uses Craven Road
3 why he walks along it every day
4 if he is the only child who does this
5 what sort of traffic uses the road
6 if he was knocked down by a car
7 if there are any traffic lights there
8 if the authorities know how dangerous it is
9 why she thinks it is so dangerous
10 if a child was killed there last month
11 where her son is now
12 if any bones were broken
13 what is wrong with him

Give the answers as well.

Transfer

You probably use a busy road every day on your way to work or to school. Describe where you cross it, what sort of traffic uses it, if there are any traffic lights there, etc.

UNIT 1

What causes headaches?
What does the policeman
suffer from?

1a

Imagine you are interviewing the policeman. Notice the two different question constructions.

> **You know that *something causes his headaches*.**
> **You ask, "What causes your headaches?"**
> **You know that *he suffers from something*.**
> **You ask, "What do you suffer from?"**

1b

Comment

1   If *what* or *who* is the subject, the *doer of the action*, do *not* use the question auxiliary (*do, does, did*).
2   But use the auxiliary if *what* or *who* is the object, and if you are using a *full verb* (not *be* or any of the modals like *can, should, must, ought to*, etc.).

1c

Now ask the policeman questions with *who* or *what*. You know that:

1   something gives him headaches
2   someone uses the road every day
3   something happens every morning
4   he does something every day
5   someone helps him when there is a traffic jam
6   he wears something when it rains
7   he does something when there is an accident

1d

Transfer

You are also interviewing a motorist. Ask various questions beginning with *who, what, what sort of,* etc. Ask:

1   what sort of petrol he uses
2   what sort of car he drives
3   who (if anybody) travels with him every morning
4   what gives him the most trouble with his car

5   who he hates most, traffic policemen or other motorists
6   what causes the traffic jams

Think of more questions you might ask about the cost, how crowded the roads are, which roads he uses to get to work, what he does when he is in a traffic jam, etc.

How many children use this
road? How many children
does Mrs Clay know?

2a

Comment

The same rule applies to *how much* and *how many*. When they go with the subject the question auxiliary is not used.

2b

Now ask the motorist questions with *how much* or *how many*. You know that:

1   other motorists use the same road
2   accidents happen on the road every day
3   he sees accidents every week
4   he knows other motorists
5   his car uses petrol
6   he spends money on his car
7   Super X Petrol costs money
8   other motorists use Super X Petrol

This policeman is directing traffic. He does this every day.

3a

Describe what you do every day or week. Talk about:

1 when you get up
2 when you go to work
3 when you have breakfast, lunch and dinner
4 what you do in the evening

3b

Now imagine that two friends of yours (we shall call them simply A and B), are discussing you. They know your daily habits.

> A: **I wonder what . . . . is doing now?**
> B: **Well (looking at his watch), it's . . . . now, so . . . . is probably . . . .ing.**

3c

Now use this 'conversation frame' for various times of the day. What would A and B say about you, for example, at:

1 7 in the morning
2 12 noon
3 3 in the afternoon
4 6 in the evening
5 8 in the evening
6 midnight
7 other important times of the day

 The problem is getting worse all the time.

4a

The present continuous form can also be used for things that *may not be going on at the actual moment you speak*. In this example it is used for something that is *in one phase of developing in the present*. Use

it yourself this way. Think of things you have read in the papers, like these:

1 There's a war on in . . . . . The people there are . . . .ing.
2 There's an economic crisis in . . . . . A lot of people are . . . . .
3 The World Football Championship is going to take place soon. The different countries are already . . . . .

4b

Think of more examples yourself. Talk about:

1 the cost of living
2 the trees and flowers at this time of the year
3 other things that are developing at the moment but may not actually be going on as you speak

5

 Active – Passive

Use the passive as Professor Campbell does here. Notice that sometimes he uses the continuous passive *(is being done)*.

> REPORTER: **Do cars cause a lot of damage?**
> CAMPBELL: **Yes, a lot of damage is caused by cars.**
> REPORTER: **Are cars destroying our cities?**
> CAMPBELL: **Yes, cities are being destroyed by cars.**

1 Do lorries use this road?
2 Are lorries using it now?
3 Do lorries make a lot of noise?
4 Is a lorry making that noise now?
5 Is Mrs Clay organising a protest march?
6 Are other people helping her?
7 So, traffic causes a lot of problems.
8 Are the police doing something about it?

Intensive Listening

2

UNIT 1

Professor Colin Campbell, whose picture is on page 8 (text 3) is being interviewed about traffic in our towns.

1

Text (shortened and adapted)

Our cities are dying physically. In most city centres some of the oldest and finest buildings are crumbling; literally falling to pieces. On the one hand, the foundations are being shaken by all the heavy traffic and, on the other hand, the bricks and mortar are being eaten away by the fumes from the traffic. It's a slow process but it's going on even though you can't see it.

Far more serious things are happening. The buildings can always be replaced but what about the air? You can hardly breathe it any more in our cities. And think of the noise. Nowadays most city centres are simply too noisy to live in. We've got to live with the motor car but we've got to become its master and not its slave.

2

Vocabulary

crumbling: falling to pieces.

literally: (here) without exaggeration.

foundations: the basis of the building.

bricks and mortar: the materials a building is made of.

fumes: the gases that come out of cars.

The buildings can be replaced: other buildings can be put in their place.

We've got to become its master and not its slave: we must learn to control it. We cannot let it control us.

3

Questions (to be answered after you have listened to the tape)

1 Why does he say our cities are dying?
2 What are the things that are causing this?
3 What sort of process is it?
4 He says there is something even more serious. What?
5 What exactly does he say about (a) the air (b) the noise?
6 Does he say the motor car is the only cause of all this?
7 What does he say we've got to do?

4

Practice

The process is going on. You can't see it.
The process is going on *even though* you can't see it.

Combine these sentences in the same way.

1 He didn't want to eat anything. He was hungry.
2 This street is very quiet. A lot of traffic uses it.
3 The building is crumbling. We've spent a lot of money on it.
4 Nobody wants to do anything about this problem. Everybody knows it is serious.
5 He didn't pass the test. He studied all weekend.

5

Discussion (and/or extended writing)

Most cities have buses and other means of public transport. Why, in your opinion, do so many people still prefer to use their own cars?

Story/Dialogue

Linda Blake is a young journalist. She is going to an interview for a job with the EBC.

1

Story

The interview was at 10 o'clock. The company's headquarters was near Marble Arch, in the centre of London.

She got on a bus at 9.15. It was a No. 79. The conductor asked for her fare. She told him she was going to Marble Arch.

"We don't go to Marble Arch. This is a 79. You want a 79A," he said. Then he told her she could catch a 79A at the next stop.

She got off and waited at the next stop. She looked at her watch. She did not have very much time. Another woman was at the stop, too. She told Linda that the 79A did not stop there but up the road.

Then she asked Linda where she wanted to go.

"Marble Arch," Linda answered. "You want an 89B, then, not a 79A!" the woman said.

Linda got on an 89B. It was now 9.45. Marble Arch was only a mile away. She asked the conductor how long it took to get there.

"It takes about half an hour this time of the day. It's all the traffic. If you're in a hurry, you ought to take the Underground or walk. It's much faster!" the conductor answered.

2

Multiple Choice

Choose the best answer: (a), (b), (c) or (d).

1 The bus came along and Linda .... it.
   (a) mounted   (b) rose   (c) got on   (d) got off
2 The fare is ....
   (a) the distance you travel   (b) the money you pay   (c) a ticket from the conductor   (d) the driver
3 She asked how long it .... to get to Marble Arch.
   (a) needed   (b) put   (c) made   (d) took

3

Questions

1 Where did Linda want to go?
2 Why did she want to go there?
3 What happened on the first bus?
4 What did Linda find out after she had got off the first bus?
5 Describe what happened on the second bus (the 89B).

 Practice

4a

Imagine the conductor said all these things to Linda. Transform them like this.

> **"You're on the wrong bus."**
> **He told her she was on the wrong bus.**

1 "You want a 79A."
2 "You can catch one at the next stop."
3 "It's faster on the Underground."
4 "It takes a long time to get there."
5 "The traffic is getting worse."

4b

Imagine the woman at the stop asked Linda these questions. Transform them like this.

> **"Where do you want to go?"**
> **She asked Linda where she wanted to go.**

1 "Which bus do you want to catch?"
2 "Where do you want to get off?"
3 "Why do you want to go to Marble Arch?"
4 "When do you have to be there?"
5 "What do you want to do there?"

5

Transfer

You are a foreign student in England. You are standing at a bus stop. A woman begins asking you questions beginning, "Why do you want ....?" "Where do you ....?" etc. Think of some of the questions. Then transform them into sentences beginning, "She asked me ...."

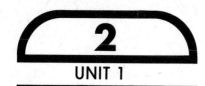

UNIT 1

(Listen to the dialogue on tape. Then use this skeleton to reproduce what Linda said.)

(Practice)

1

Dialogue
On the 79
CONDUCTOR: Fares, please. Any more fares?
LINDA: ....
CONDUCTOR: You're on the wrong bus. We don't go to Marble Arch.
LINDA: .... you? I thought ....
CONDUCTOR: No. This is a 79. You want a 79A.
LINDA: ....? Where .... one?
CONDUCTOR: Get off at the next stop.
Waiting at the stop
LINDA: .... me. .... know .... the 79A .... here?
WOMAN: The 79A? No, it stops up the road.
LINDA: But a conductor told me .... here.
WOMAN: Oh, don't believe what those conductors tell you, dear. They don't know what they're talking about. Where d'you want to go, then?
LINDA: Marble Arch. And .... much time, ...
WOMAN: Marble Arch? You want an 89B, then. Look! One's coming now!
On the 89B
CONDUCTOR: Fares, please.
LINDA: .... please. Uh, you *do* .... Marble Arch, ...?
CONDUCTOR: That's right. Four please.
LINDA: How long .... to get there?
CONDUCTOR: Oh, it takes about half an hour this time of the day.
LINDA: ....? But .... only a mile ....
CONDUCTOR: Yes, but it's all the traffic. If you're in a hurry, you ought to take the Underground or walk. It's much faster!

2a

Listen carefully to Linda's intonation here.

I CONDUCTOR: **We don't go to Marble Arch.**
  LINDA: **Don't you? I thought you did.**

Answer these statements in the same way.
1 These buses don't go to Marble Arch.
2 That isn't the right fare.
3 Those aren't English pennies.
4 This bus doesn't stop here.
5 You aren't on the right bus.
6 You don't know how to do this exercise.

2b

Linda did not say to the woman at the stop:

I **"Does the 79A stop here?" Instead she said: "Excuse me. Do you know if the 79A stops here?"**

Ask these questions in the same way.
1 Does this bus go to Marble Arch?
2 Is it 10 o'clock yet?
3 How often does the 79A run?
4 Do other buses go to Marble Arch?
5 Is Marble Arch near here?

3

Transfer
You are at a railway station in London. You want to go to York (a city in Yorkshire). You want to know when the next train leaves, if there is a dining car on the train, etc. Think of all the questions you might ask. What exactly would you say?

Grammar Summary/Revision

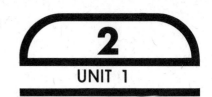

REPORTED QUESTIONS

Basic situation 1a Suppose a girl like Linda asked you various questions. Now, the day after, you are telling a friend about these questions. Observe the difference in form and tense between the question Linda actually asked and the way you report it afterwards.

"Does the 79A stop on the corner?"	**She asked if the 79A stopped on the corner.**
"Where does the 79A stop?"	**She asked where the 79A stopped.**
"How far away is Marble Arch?"	**She asked how far away Marble Arch was.**

Now do the same. Report these questions to a friend. Linda asked them yesterday.

1 "When does the next bus arrive?"
2 "Where does the 79A go?"
3 "Why do buses stop running at night?"
4 "Where is Marble Arch?"
5 "How long does it take to get there?"
6 "Do many buses go there?"
7 "What's the fare?"
8 "Is there a cheaper way to get there?"

Comment 1b
1 As in all reported speech, the present (*is*) is transformed to the past (*was*).
2 The question auxiliary (*do/does*) is not used in the reported question. Thus, "Does it stop here?" becomes "She asked if it stopped here".
3 Observe in particular the position of the verb *be* in reported questions with *where*, *how* far, etc. (She asked where Marble Arch *was*.)

EXTENDED WRITING

2 Suppose you are a young journalist. You want a job with the same company that Linda Blake wants to work for. Its name is:

The English Broadcasting Company,
6 Mortimer Street,
London W.1.

Write a short letter to say who you are and applying for the job. These are the facts.

1 You saw an advertisement for the job in *The Times*.
2 You are now working for the *Harlow Herald* (a small town newspaper in Essex).
3 You speak French and German.
4 You are very interested in making educational programmes.
5 You have never made educational programmes before.
6 You would like more details about the job.

Begin the letter: Dear Sirs,
Finish it with: Yours faithfully,

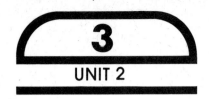

3
UNIT 2

THE ENGLISH BROADCASTING COMPANY

1

This is the headquarters of the English Broadcasting Company. People call it the EBC for short. This company makes radio and television programmes in English and then sells them to countries all over the world.

Questions

1 What is this building?
2 What does EBC mean?
3 What does the EBC do?

2

Hello. My name's David Nelson. I was born in England but I lived in South America when I was a child. I lived there for ten years. Then I came back to England. I'm a journalist. I worked for a London newspaper for five years, and I've been working in television for the past two years. I don't work for the EBC. I work for another company. The EBC has just offered me a job. I'm thinking about the offer. I'm considering it very carefully.

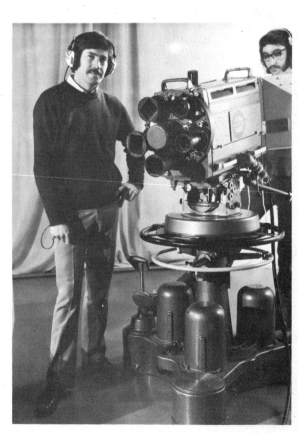

Questions

Ask and answer questions about David like this:
Ask where he was born.

> A: Where was he born?
> B: In England.

Now you do it. Construct the questions carefully. Be careful of the tense! Ask:

1 what his name is
2 where he lived when he was a child
3 how long he lived there
4 where he lives now
5 what his job is
6 if he still works for a London paper
7 how long he worked for the paper
8 what he has been doing for the past two years

3

My name's Linda Blake. I was born and brought up in a small town. I studied at Cambridge for three years. Then I became a teacher. I was a teacher for three years. For the last year I've been working for a women's magazine. I'm trying to get a job with the EBC. I don't think I'll get it because I have no experience in television. I like my job with the magazine but I'd like one with the EBC even more!

Questions

Ask and answer questions about Linda. Find out:

1 where she was born
2 if she was brought up there
3 how long she studied at university
4 what she did then
5 how long she did it
6 who she is working for now
7 how long she has been working for the magazine
8 what sort of job she wants
9 if she thinks she'll get it
10 if she likes her present job

4

My name's Robert Wilson. I'm the director of educational programmes for the EBC. In other words, I direct the programmes and other people write them. I offered David Nelson a job last week. As you see, I'm having an interview with Linda Blake now. She hasn't got any experience in television but I like her. I think she'll probably get the job.

Questions

Answer these questions with short "tags"; like this.

A: Who makes educational programmes?
B: The EBC *does*.

1 Who is the director of educational programmes for the EBC?
2 Who writes them?
3 Who directs the programmes?
4 Who offered David Nelson a job last week?
5 Who's sitting in Wilson's office now?
6 Who's having an interview with Linda?
7 Who will probably get the job?

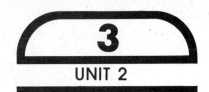

UNIT 2

The contrast between the simple past and the present perfect

1a

You are talking to Linda Blake. Notice the questions you ask her.

> LINDA: **I lived in France for a time.**
> YOU: **Oh? How long did you live there?**
>
> LINDA: **I live in the north of London.**
> YOU: **Oh, how long have you been living there?**

Now you do it!

1 I worked in a factory once.
2 I work for a women's magazine now.
3 I stayed at the London Hilton once.
4 I studied German at school.
5 I'm learning Spanish.
6 I'm looking for another job.
7 I had a wonderful job once.
8 I was very ill.
9 I watched television last night.
10 Shh! I'm watching a television programme.

1b

Study the diagram. Notice the division of time into three blocks.

Past   Past to Present   Present

David worked for a London paper for five years.

He is still working in television.

He has been working in television for the past two years.

1c

Comment

1 The past simple is used here for lengths of time completely in the past. They do not connect with the present in any way.
2 The present perfect form here (*has been working for . . .*) connects past with present. For example, "He started working in television two years ago. He is still working in television. He has been working in television for two years."

1d

Transfer

Think back to the past. Describe things you did over a certain period but *which are over now*. Some of these questions may help you.

1 Describe where you went to school and how long for.
2 Have you had more than one job in your life? Describe the job or jobs you *had* before your present one. Say how long you had it.
3 Have you had more than one car or motor bike in your life? Describe some of the ones you had before. How long did you have them?
4 Have you ever had an illness that lasted a long time? Describe it.

Verbs that rarely take the continuous

2a

Basic situation

Linda and Wilson are talking. He is interviewing her. The interview is *described in the past. Describe it in the present.* It is going on now. Notice that some verbs do *not* take the continuous. Transform like this.

> **Linda sat in a chair.**
> **Linda is sitting in a chair.**
>
> **Wilson needed another reporter.**
> **Wilson needs another reporter.**

1 Linda looked for a job.
2 She wanted one with the EBC.
3 She thought she had talent.
4 Wilson believed her.
5 He asked a lot of questions.
6 She told him about herself.
7 Wilson listened carefully.
8 He saw she had blue eyes.
9 He explained the job to her.
10 He liked her.
11 She watched him.
12 She saw some pictures behind him.
13 She looked at them.
14 She heard a knock at the door.
15 She listened to the secretary.
16 She understood everything.

2b

Comment

1 Verbs of opinion *(believe, like, doubt)* rarely take the continuous.
2 Neither do the verbs of perception *(see, hear, know, understand)*.
3 Note that when the action of seeing or hearing is directly under the control of the person mentioned, we use *look at* and *listen to*. These have continuous forms. You can stop looking at or listening to something if you want to. You cannot do the same with *see* and *hear*.

Verbs that can change their meaning

3a

The verbs here are used with different meanings. In one meaning they can take the continuous. In the other they cannot. Transform from past to present. Imagine all these things are going on now.

1 Wilson had lunch with David Nelson.
2 Nelson had a lot of experience.
3 He thought about the offer.
4 He thought it was a good offer.
5 He considered it a very good offer.
6 He considered it carefully.
7 Linda had no experience in television.
8 She had an interview with Wilson.
9 He thought she had talent.
10 He thought about some other people.

3b

Comment

1 *Think* and *consider* can be verbs of opinion. In this sense they occur in the simple form.
2 *Think* and *consider* can also mean *to give attention to* or *to go over in one's mind.* In this sense they often take the continuous.
3 *Have* can often describe an action, as in *They're having lunch.* In this sense it replaces another verb, like *eat*, and can take the continuous.
4 *Have* in the sense in which it is used in sentences like: *He has a lot of experience* or *She has a new car* is used in the simple form.

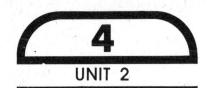

UNIT 2

A young reporter talks about the different kinds of newspapers in England.

1

Text (shortened and adapted)

Every journalist wants to work on one of the big national newspapers but most of us have to start on a small local paper. Local papers circulate in a town or a particular area. They have small circulations, perhaps only a few thousand readers. National papers circulate throughout the whole country and may have circulations of eight million readers.

There are two types of national papers, the "quality papers" and the "popular papers". In a popular paper you may see a girl in a bathing suit or even less on the second page and the news often has a different angle to it. It is often more sensational.

A few years ago a driving examiner refused to give a girl a driving test. He said her skirt was too short. In one of the popular papers this story was on the front page. Eight paragraphs were written about it and there was also a picture of the girl. In one of the quality papers the story was on a back page and only two paragraphs were written about it.

2

Vocabulary

circulate: is bought and read.

circulation: the number of people who buy the paper.

the news has a different angle: the news is treated in a different way.

sensational: presented so that it causes as much interest and excitement as possible.

driving examiner: the person who gives a driving test to new drivers before they can get a licence.

3

Questions (to be answered after you have listened to the tape)

1 What is the main difference between local and national papers?
2 What are the two main types of national papers?
3 What sort of things will you see in a popular paper?
4 Is the news different in any way?
5 Tell the story of the girl in the short skirt in your own words.
6 Describe the way the two types of paper treated this story.

4

Practice

What are the missing words or phrases?

1 National papers may .... of eight million readers.
2 National papers .... the whole country.
3 The news in a popular paper often .... to it.
4 A few years .... a driving examiner .... a girl a .... test.
5 In the popular paper, eight paragraphs .... this story.

5

Discussion (and/or extended writing)

1 Imagine you are in a dentist's waiting room. The dentist is going to pull out some of your teeth. Which of the two types of paper would you prefer to read before you go in to see him? Why?
2 Describe in English a piece of news you have heard or read recently.

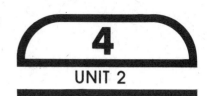

Linda Blake has an interview with Robert Wilson.

1

Story

Linda was a few minutes late. Wilson had left the office when she got there. His secretary told her he would be back in a few minutes. She had to sit down and wait for a few minutes in the outer office.

"I'll never get this job," she told herself. For a moment she wanted to run out of the building. Just then, Wilson came through the door and hurried into his office. A few seconds later his secretary took Linda in and introduced her.

Linda apologised for being late. Wilson did not seem to mind. They chatted casually for a few seconds and then got down to business. He took out her letter of application.

"You've never worked in radio or television before, have you?" he said. Linda answered that she was afraid she hadn't. Now she was even more sure that she would not get the job. Wilson asked her a few more questions.

To her surprise he seemed impressed with her other qualifications. She was even more surprised when he asked her if she could start soon. "I wonder if you'd mind starting next month?" he asked with a smile. It seemed she had got the job after all!

2

Multiple Choice

Choose the best answer: (a), (b), (c) or (d).

1   To chat casually means to talk . . . .
   (a) about causes   (b) informally and easily
   (c) foolishly   (d) about business
2   Wilson *was impressed* with her qualifications.
   He . . . . them.
   (a) liked   (b) looked carefully at   (c) did not
   understand   (d) was interested in
3   She had got the job *after all*. She had got it
   after . . . .
   (a) a long time   (b) many other people
   (c) thinking she would not get it   (d) the talk

3

Questions

1   Why did Linda have to wait?
2   What did Wilson's secretary say?
3   Why did she want to run away?
4   What happened then?
5   Describe what happened during the interview.
6   Why was Linda surprised at the end?

Practice

4a

What do you think Linda and Wilson said when they were introduced? What exactly do you think Linda said when she "apologised for being late"?

4b

Notice how what Linda said to herself is transformed in this pattern.

| **"I'll never get the job."**
She was sure she would never get the job.

Transform these thoughts of Linda's in the same way. Begin, "She was sure . . ."

1   "I won't have a chance."
2   "I'll say something stupid."
3   "They'll give the job to someone else."
4   "I'll do something foolish during the interview."
5   "Wilson won't like me."

4c

Transform this pattern.

| **"I've never worked in radio."**
She said she had never worked in radio.

1   "I've never done this sort of work."
2   "I've always wanted to do it."
3   "I've written lots of articles."
4   "I've been a journalist for a year."
5   "I've always been interested in television."

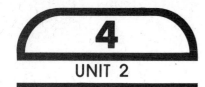

UNIT 2

Dialogue/Practice

First, listen to the tape. Then reproduce *Linda's* part.

Practice

1

Dialogue
Wilson's secretary is introducing Linda
SECRETARY: Mr Wilson, this is Miss Blake.
WILSON: How do you do.
LINDA: ....
WILSON: Thank you, Margaret. Well, Miss Blake, do sit down, won't you?
LINDA: .... I hope .... excuse me .... late.
WILSON: Oh, that's all right. I suppose you had difficulty in finding the building.
LINDA: No, that .... it. It .... traffic.
WILSON: Oh, yes. Of course. It's very heavy at this time of the day.
LINDA: Yes, ... Very ....
WILSON: Yes, well, don't worry about it. Now, I have your letter of application here. I'd like to ask you a few questions.
LINDA: ....
WILSON: You've never worked in radio or television before, have you?
LINDA: No, ... afraid ..... But I *have* .... a women's magazine .... year.
WILSON: Yes, I see that. Now, you were also a teacher for a time.
LINDA: Yes, ... secondary school .... three years.
WILSON: Uh huh. Now tell me why you're interested in this sort of job.
Ten minutes later. They are still talking
WILSON: So, you started writing articles a year ago.
LINDA: Well, in fact, ... articles before then.
WILSON: Oh, had you?
LINDA: Yes, ... some when .... still a teacher.
WILSON: I see. Yes. You're just the sort of person we need.
LINDA: You mean, ... chance I'll .... the job?
WILSON: Yes, I think there is. In fact, I wonder if you'd mind starting next month?
LINDA: ....
WILSON: Yes. Is that too soon?
LINDA: No, ...! .... very much!

2a

Linda was late. She said:

▌ **"I hope you'll excuse me for being late."**

What do you say if you are at a party and you:
1 arrive late
2 spill wine on the carpet
3 break the window
4 disturb the neighbours
5 wake the baby
6 ruin the party
Apologise in the same way for other terrible things you might do.

2b

Answer as Wilson does here, always beginning, "Yes, I think ...."

▌ LINDA: **You mean, there's a chance I'll get the job?**
▌ WILSON: **Yes, I think there is.**

1 You mean, perhaps I'll get the job?
2 So you think I'm the right person?
3 You like my qualifications?
4 And you think I can do the work?
5 You mean, you're going to give me the job?

2c

At the end Wilson said:

▌ **"I wonder if you'd mind starting next month?"**

Use this pattern to ask Linda to:
1 take a typing test
2 come back tomorrow
3 answer a few personal questions
4 wait a moment
5 do some work today

3

Transfer
Imagine you are interviewing a secretary. You want to know about her typing, previous jobs, etc. What questions do you ask?

Grammar Summary/Revision

THE PAST PERFECT

1a   Note Linda's answer here.

WILSON: **So you started writing articles a year ago.**
LINDA: **Well, in fact, I'd written articles before that.**

Comment **1b**   **1** Use the past perfect (*had done*) when you are already speaking about the past (*You started writing articles a year ago*) and you want to step *still further* into the past (*I'd written articles before then*).

2 As we have seen the past perfect is also used in reported speech. *Has done* (present perfect) becomes *had done*.

1c   Now make sentences with the pattern *had already done when* . . . : like this.

Wilson went out at 3. Linda got there at 3.05.
Wilson had already gone out when Linda got there.

1 The film started at 8. We got there at 8.15.
2 The rain stopped at noon. We went out a few minutes later.
3 The bus left on time. I got to the bus station late.
4 Wilson interviewed five people on Monday and saw Linda on Tuesday.
5 I finished breakfast and you came in a few minutes later.
6 I fell asleep and a few minutes later the phone rang.

EXTENDED WRITING
(and/or oral practice)

2a   Describe yourself in the same way that Linda and David described themselves on pages 16 and 17. Answer these questions. Where were you born? What sort of school did you go to? What did you study there? How long did you work in various jobs before your present one? What sort of work did you do? How long have you been working in your present job? What do you think of it? Are you satisfied with it? Why are you learning English? What sort of work would you like to do later?

2b   Now imagine you are being interviewed for a new job. Write the interview out as a dialogue.

5 Space travel

This is part of a television programme that Robert Wilson and his team did. It is about space travel.

1

This is the planet earth. It looks rather strange because we are looking at it from the moon. It has just risen above the moon's horizon.

Of course, very few people have ever seen it from the moon, but most people have seen photographs like this. Such photographs don't tell us anything new. We've known for hundreds of years that the earth is round, like a ball. But in the past, people believed it was flat.

Questions

Ask and answer questions like this:
Ask what this is.

    A: What's this?
    B: It's the planet earth.

Ask:
1 why it looks so strange
2 what the earth has just done
3 how many people have seen the earth from the moon
4 how many people have seen such photographs
5 how long we have known that the earth is round
6 what people believed in the past

2

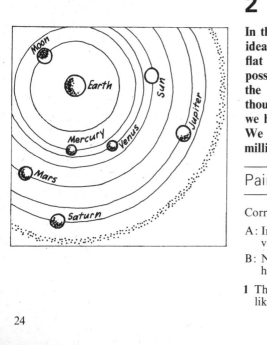

In the past, people used to have all sorts of strange ideas. They used to think that the earth was like a flat board. They were absolutely certain that it was possible to fall off the end. They used to believe that the earth was the centre of the universe. They thought the sun moved round the earth. Of course, we have known for a long time that this is not so. We are a small planet in a huge universe, among a million stars.

Paired Practice

Correct A's statements, as B does.

A: In the past people used to have very few strange ideas.
B: No, you're wrong. They used to have all sorts of strange ideas.

1 They used to believe the earth was like a round ball.
2 They didn't really think it was possible to fall off the end.
3 They knew the earth moved round the sun.
4 We've known for only a few years that this isn't so.
5 We're a large planet in a small universe.

24

3

This rocket has just taken off. It is going to Mars. Scientists have been sending space craft there for several years now. About 100 years ago an astronomer looked at Mars through his telescope and said he could see canals there. Ever since he did that, people have been asking the same question: "Is there life on Mars?"

Questions

Ask and answer:

1 what has just happened in this picture
2 where the rocket is going
3 how long scientists have been sending space craft there
4 an astronomer did something 100 years ago; ask what!
5 what people have been doing since he did that

4

Men have been interested in the stars ever since they first looked up into the sky. Some of these stars may have their own planets. If that is so, we can suppose that intelligent life may exist on one of them. The problem is that the nearest star is four light years away. In other words, light from it has been travelling for four years when it finally reaches us. Probably nobody from earth will ever visit that star because it would take a rocket a hundred thousand years to reach it.

Questions

Answer these questions. Use the language of the text.

1 How long have men been interested in the stars?
2 What may some of these stars have?
3 What can we suppose if some stars have their own planets?
4 What is the problem?
5 Imagine light from the nearest star has just reached us; what has been happening?
6 Why, in all probability, will no one from earth ever visit that star?

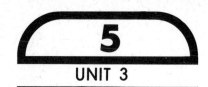

UNIT 3

> We *have known* this for years.
> We *have been doing* this for years.

1

Respond as B does here.

> A: **Scientists know there's no life on the moon.**
> B: **They've known that for years!**
>
> A: **They often send rockets there.**
> B: **They've been sending rockets there for years!**

1 They have rockets now.
2 But they often have trouble with them.
3 They're trying to improve them.
4 They believe there's life on other planets.
5 They often study other stars.
6 They think some of them have planets.
7 They sometimes get radio signals from outer space.
8 They know there's life out there, somewhere!
9 They often think about things like this.
10 They're working on the problem.

2a

Men *have been interested* in the stars ever since they

past   to   present

first *looked* up into the sky.
      past

Notice how the present perfect is used here for something that started with an action in the past and is still true in the present. Notice also how the action in the past that was the starting point is in the simple past tense. Now make sentences for these situations: like this.

> **I'm interested in space travel. I read a book about it once.**
> **I've been interested in space travel ever since I read a book about it.**

1 My son wants to become an astronaut. He saw a film about them.
2 I have a terrible cold. I got wet in the rain.
3 I'm looking for a job. I lost my old one.
4 Linda is very happy. She got a job with the EBC.
5 Linda's father is in hospital. He had a bad accident.
6 I'm feeling ill. I ate some strange fish.

2b

Transfer

There must be many things which you *have been doing* for some time now and which *began* with some action in the past. For example, perhaps you got a new job and are earning more money now. You could say:

> **I've been earning more money ever since I got this new job.**

Think of more such examples! Here are some situations to help you but you must also think of some of your own.

1 You bought a car some time ago. You're always short of money now.
2 You started learning English. Now you listen to English programmes on the radio and buy English newspapers.

People used to believe that the earth was flat.

3a

This form, as you probably already know, is used for things that people did in the past but no longer do. Now read this short story.

George Mellor was my friend a few years ago. He isn't my friend any more. A few years ago he was poor. Now he's rich. When I knew him he wore shabby clothes, was very thin and lived in a small flat. He rode a bicycle. He was an art student. He always said, "Some day I'm going to be a great artist!" Then he met Priscilla. Priscilla has a very rich father. George married her. Now he wears expensive clothes, is rather fat and lives in a huge house. He drives a fast sports car now. He's what they call a "company director". Now he says, "Some day I'm going to be Prime Minister!" Oh, well. Life is good for some people.

3b

Now, from this story, make at least seven sentences like this:

George used to be my friend. He used to be an .... but now .....

3c

Now form questions like this:

A: **Did George really *use* to be your friend?**
B: **Yes, he *did*, but he *isn't* any more.**
A: **And did he really *use* to go to art school?**
B: **Yes, he *did*, but he *doesn't* any more.**

Now you do it. With someone else, take the part of A: the other person is B.

3d

Transfer

David Nelson is now a successful journalist. Only a few years ago he was a young, very poor journalist. He earned very little money. Think of all the things he used to do then, the way he used to live, the sort of car he used to drive, etc. Is your own life very different from the way you used to live five or ten years ago? Describe what you used to do then.

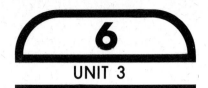

6

UNIT 3

> An astronomer talks about Mars.

1

Text (shortened and adapted)

In 1877 an Italian astronomer named Schiaparelli noticed some dark markings on the surface of Mars. He called them 'canali', which, by the way, doesn't necessarily mean canals in English. Later an American named Lowell studied these markings. He said that they were canals and that intelligent beings had put them there. Since then other astronomers with better equipment have also been observing Mars and they haven't seen any canals there. Since 1965 we've also had fairly good photographs of the surface of Mars. We got them from a space probe, *Mariner 4*. It went past Mars and sent back photographs and measurements. Since 1971 we've had even better photographs from another space probe. There might be primitive plant life there but there is no intelligent life there, nor any green monsters with eyes in the middle of their foreheads, either.

2

Vocabulary

markings: lines, marks, etc, which may or may not be man-made.

intelligent beings: some form of intelligent life.

equipment: machines and other aids which people use in their work.

space probe: rocket sent into space to collect information.

primitive: very very simple.

monsters: terrible unusual animals.

3

Questions (to be answered after you have listened to the tape)

1 How long have people been talking about these 'canals'?
2 What exactly did Schiaparelli do?
3 Who was Lowell and what did he do?
4 What have astronomers since then been doing and what have they said?
5 How long have we had good photographs of Mars?
6 What was *Mariner 4* and what did it do?
7 What kind of life might there be on Mars?
8 What kind of life definitely does not exist there?

    Practice

4a

Imagine an astronaut from another planet has just landed on the earth (a planet his culture has been observing for a long time through telescopes). Describe what he sees and what happens *from his point of view.*

4b

Both the present perfect (*has done*) and the past simple (*did*) usually become the past perfect (*had done*) in reported speech.

> Lowell said intelligent beings *had put* the canals there.
> Lowell's exact words were probably,
> "Intelligent beings *have put* (or *put*) the canals there."

Now put these statements of Lowell into reported speech. Begin, "Lowell said that . . ."

1 "Mars was like the earth once."
2 "Perhaps it had rivers and oceans."
3 "Most of the water has gone."
4 "It has become a dry, dead place."
5 "But perhaps there was life there once."
6 "All that life has probably died."

The EBC offered David Nelson a job in Robert Wilson's team. David decided to accept.

1

Story

David picked up the phone. He wanted to tell Wilson that he would take the job. He dialled the EBC. Their switchboard operator answered. She asked him if he knew Wilson's extension. He didn't, and neither did she. It took her several seconds to find it. But when she put David through, it was not to the right Wilson. It seemed there was also a George Wilson at the EBC. He told David that he would get the switchboard for him. Then, suddenly, David was cut off. The line went dead.

David was beginning to feel irritated now. He quickly dialled again. He got the wrong number. His irritation grew. He dialled a third time. This time he got the EBC but the operator told him Wilson's line was engaged. David slammed the phone down angrily. Only a moment later, it rang. He picked it up and shouted "Hello" into it. It was Robert Wilson.

"I tried to phone you a moment ago," David told Robert Wilson.

"Really? So did I! I mean, I tried to phone you, but your line was engaged," Wilson answered.

2

Multiple Choice

1 If you want to phone someone you must first
   .... the number.
   (a) choose   (b) select   (c) dial   (d) make
2 The switchboard operator is the telephonist in
   a large firm who .... to the person you want.
   (a) relates   (b) puts you through   (c) contacts
   you   (d) binds you
3 David did not know Wilson's extension and
   .... did the switchboard operator.
   (a) neither   (b) not   (c) so   (d) also
4 If you are *irritated*, you are ....
   (a) bored   (b) tired   (c) helpless   (d) angry

3

Questions

1 Why did David want to phone Wilson?
2 Describe all the trouble he had the first time he
   rang.
3 What happened the second time?
4 What happened the third time?
5 What did Wilson tell David?

Practice

4a

Someone asks you, "Do you know ....?" You don't. What is a *polite* answer?

4b

Put these things the operator says to David into sentences beginning, "She told him . . ." or "She asked him if . . ."

> **"Can you phone later?"**
> **She asked him if he could phone later.**
> **"Mr Wilson isn't here."**
> **She told him Wilson was not there.**

1 "His line is engaged."
2 "Will you phone later?"
3 "Do you want Robert Wilson or George
   Wilson?"
4 "Robert Wilson is out."
5 "His secretary is in."
6 "Do you want to speak to his secretary?"
7 "What's your name, please?"
8 "Are you phoning from London?"
9 "His extension is 45."

4c

These things were expressed in single sentences. How?

1 He didn't know. She didn't know.
2 She found it. It took several seconds.
3 Then she put David through. But it was not to
   the right Wilson.

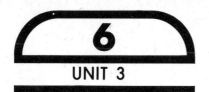

Dialogue/Practice

First, listen to the dialogue and then use this skeleton to reproduce what *David* says.

David has just phoned the EBC
OPERATOR: Good morning. EBC.
DAVID: .... Robert Wilson ....
OPERATOR: Do you know the extension?
DAVID: .... afraid ....
OPERATOR: One moment. I'll put you through.
DAVID: .... My name .... I'd ....
SECRETARY: One moment.
MAN: Good morning.
DAVID: .... Robert Wilson?
MAN: No, this is George Wilson. Robert Wilson's in another department. You've got the wrong extension.
DAVID: ....
MAN: I'll get the switchboard for you.
Suddenly David is cut off
DAVID: Good Lord! .... off!
He dials again
VOICE: Hello?
DAVID: .... EBC? I .... a moment ago.
VOICE: What number did you want?
DAVID: .... 2672, the ....
VOICE: This is 2627. You've got the wrong number!
DAVID: Oh, ...
He dials again
OPERATOR: EBC. Good morning.
DAVID: .... to speak to ....
OPERATOR: I'm sorry. His line is engaged. Can you wait?
DAVID: No! .... later!
After a moment his *phone rings*
DAVID: ....?
WILSON: Hello? Is that David Nelson? This is Robert Wilson.
DAVID: ....! .... a moment ago!
WILSON: Really? So did I! I mean, I phoned *you* a moment ago, but your line was engaged.

Practice

2a

Answer as David does here, with "No, I'm afraid ...." use the same intonation!

> OPERATOR: **Do you know the extension?**
> DAVID: **No, I'm afraid I don't.**

1 Can you phone later?
2 Do you understand everything?
3 Is my voice clear?
4 Did you understand me a second ago?
5 Have you got my number?
6 Is your phone working?

2b

Notice the use of *so* and *neither* here.

> DAVID: **I phoned a moment ago.**
> WILSON: *So* **did I!**
> DAVID: **I didn't get the right number.**
> WILSON: *Neither* **did I!**

Now answer as Wilson did.
1 I got the wrong number.
2 I didn't get the right number.
3 I don't understand.
4 I can't hear anything.
5 Now I can hear better.
6 I have a lot of trouble with the phone.
7 I'm not satisfied.
8 I'm very angry!

3

Transfer

Wilson and David are on the phone. They want to meet for lunch. They can't find a convenient time and the line is poor. They can't understand each other. They both say, "I'm afraid I can't/it isn't etc." and "Neither/So....". Imagine parts of the dialogue.

Grammar Summary/Revision

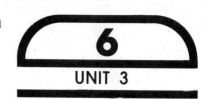

6

UNIT 3

**REPORTED SPEECH
REVIEW AND SUMMARY**

1a   Observe the tense change from direct to reported (indirect) speech.

Direct speech	Indirect speech
1 "These canals *are* part of a huge water system."	He said that the canals *were* part of a huge water system.
2 "You *can* see them through a telescope."	He said you *could* see them through a telescope.
3 "Intelligent beings *put* them there."	He said intelligent beings *had put* them there.
4 "Mars *has* probably *lost* most of its water."	He said Mars *had* probably *lost* most of its water.

Comment **1b**

Direct speech	Indirect speech
1 present ——— becomes ——→	past (after *said, told,* etc.)
2 *may, can, will, must, shall, is going to* (modals)	*might, could, would, had to, should, was going to*
3 past	past perfect (or past)
4 present perfect	past perfect

EXTENDED WRITING
(and/or oral practice)

2   Write either a dialogue or an excerpt from a novel for the following situation.

Basic situation: Robert Wilson wants to phone Bill Hartman, head of the educational department of Radio Station WRPAX, in San Francisco, California, USA. The number is 066–765500.

Happenings:

1 Robert has to dial 100 and tell the operator he wants "International Services". She puts him through.

2 The international operator asks him what country he wants and then puts him through to still another operator.

3 He gives the number. The operator does not understand at first and he has to repeat it several times.

4 When he gets the number in San Francisco the switchboard operator puts him through to the wrong extension. A man named Bill Cartwright answers. Cartwright tries to get the switchboard operator.

5 Wilson is suddenly cut off. He has to explain to the operator in London what has happened.

6 He gets the number again and, this time, the right extension. Bill Hartman's secretary answers. Hartman has just gone to lunch.

Education

1

The man in this picture is not a teacher, so he must be a pupil. The boy next to him is learning to read and write, so the man must be learning to read and write, too.

Formal education often ends as soon as people reach a certain age. But a lot of men and women are going back to school. Some are only continuing their education. Others, like this man, are only just beginning it.

Questions

You are interviewing a teacher about this picture. These are his answers; find questions for them.

1 No, he's a pupil, too.
2 To read and write.
3 No, they both are doing that.
4 As soon as people reach a certain age.
5 A lot are.
6 No, he isn't. He's only just beginning it.

2

People can go on learning until they are eighty or ninety. There is really no age limit. This woman must be at least fifty. She is learning a foreign language.

People are never too old to learn. It really is true that we can go on learning until the day we die.

Questions

Find questions for these answers.

1 Until they're eighty or ninety.
2 No, there really isn't.
3 At least fifty.
4 A foreign language.
5 No, they're never too old.
6 Yes, it really is true.

Answer these questions, using the language of the text.
1 What used to happen in the past?
2 How long did children go on repeating things?
3 What do many teachers wonder today?
4 What do these teachers say?

3

Children's education is changing very rapidly today. In the past, teachers made children sit still for hours. They made them memorise all sorts of things. In other words, the children had to go on repeating things until they knew them "by heart". Today, many teachers wonder if it is possible to make children learn at all. They say you can only help them learn. They say you must let children learn and discover things for themselves.

Paired Practice

Ask other people in the class about their school days. Ask questions like, "Did your teacher make you sit still for hours?" etc.

4

But for these children, school is a kind of prison. They are there only because their parents make them go. They get out of the classroom as soon as the teacher lets them leave. Many of them want to find jobs but the law will not let them work until they reach a certain age. And so, they have to stay in school. Often they do not learn anything at all and hate every moment.

Questions

a
1 Why do these children go to school if they hate it so much?
2 When do they get out of the classroom?
3 Why don't they find jobs now?
4 How much do they learn?
5 How do they feel about school?

b
You are interviewing some of these children. Ask them:
1 why they go to school
2 if they stay in school longer than they have to
3 if they want to find jobs now
4 why they don't do this
5 if they learn a lot in school
6 if they like school very much
Give the answers as well.

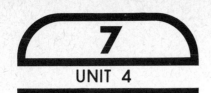

UNIT 4

Subordinators *until, as soon as*, etc.

Must used to express assumptions

1a

Until and *as soon as* are typical examples of subordinators. (Others are *if, before, after*.) Observe the tense in the clause that follows them.

> A: **Wait here. I'll be back in a few minutes.**
> B: **All right. I'll wait *until* you *get* back.**
>
> A: **The train's going to stop soon. We must get out immediately.**
> B: **All right. I'll get out *as soon as* it *stops*.**

1b

1   *Until* indicates how long the action of waiting *will go on*.
2   *As soon as* indicates when the action of 'getting out' *will start*.

1c

Now answer as B does. Use either *until* or *as soon as*.

1   The bell's going to ring soon. You must go into class immediately.
2   Stay under this tree. The rain's going to stop soon.
3   Watch this television programme. It's going to end soon.
4   The lesson's going to end soon. Come out then.
5   Stay with me for a few minutes. I think I'll feel better soon.
6   Mary's going to come soon. Wait for her!
7   Study this carefully. Then you'll understand it!
8   Finish that homework! Then come out with me.

1d

Transfer

Imagine you are listening to a long and boring lecture. You are hungry. You want a drink. You want to get up and stretch your legs but you can't leave. You have to hear the whole lecture.

1   Describe some of the things you will do *as soon as* the lecture ends.
2   Describe some of the things you have to do *until* the lecture ends.

2a

Two people, A and B, are talking about the photograph for Text 1. Notice B's responses.

> A: **The man in this picture isn't a teacher. The boy's a pupil.**
> B: **Then the man *must* be a pupil, too.**
>
> A: **That boy is learning to read and write.**
> B: **Then the man *must* be learning to read and write, too.**

2b

Comment

B uses *must* here for what he *supposes* is true.
Notice that *must*, like all modals, can also be used with a continuous form (*must be learning*).

2c

Now, answer as B did.

1 I wonder what nationality the man is. The boy next to him is Italian.
2 The boy is also learning to count.
3 The boy's seat is very hard.
4 The boy is learning English.
5 He's doing English exercises.
6 The boy lives in a small town in the south of Italy.
7 The boy does a lot of homework every day.

2d

Transfer

Now, think of somebody you know very well but who is not with you now. Think of that person's daily activities and then make sentences with *must be . . . .ing* like this.

"I have a friend. He works in a factory from 8 to 4. It's 9 o'clock now. He *must be working* in the factory at this moment."

3a

1	2	3
Make		
	someone	do
Let		

Comment

1 Notice that after *let* or *make*, the verb in box 3 is always the *infinitive* (*do* and not *to do*).
2 Any pronoun in box 2 must, of course, be in the objective case (*me, them,* etc.).

3b

Now study this conversation. Two women are talking about their school days fifty years ago.

> A: **When I was at school, we had to do a lot of homework.**
> B: **Yes, our teachers** *made us* **do a lot of homework, too.**
> A: **And we never took an active part in the lessons.**
> B: **No, our teachers** *never let us* **take an active part in the lessons, either.**

3c

Now answer as B does, using sentences with *never let us* or *made us*.

1 When I was at school, we worked very hard.
2 We never talked in class.
3 We bought lots of books.
4 We stood up when the teachers came in.
5 We didn't play games.
6 We did lots of homework.
7 We never came late.
8 We never criticised the teachers.

3d

Transfer

Think of things your teachers or parents *made you do* when you went to school.
What didn't they *let you do*?
What are some of the things you think we should *let children do* in modern schools which they couldn't do before?

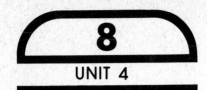

8

UNIT 4

Two people are interviewed about their ideas on education. One is an ordinary "man in the street". The other is an educational psychologist.

1

Text (shortened and adapted)

The man in the street

When I was at school, I hated it. I couldn't stand it. I wasn't happy until I got out. I think this idea of permanent education is crazy. I know some people go back to school when they're older . . . go to language classes at the local "tech" and all that . . . but I can't understand people who want to spend all their lives in school.

The educational psychologist

The idea of permanent education is practical because we're never really too old to go on learning. Of course, there are certain limits, but they aren't age limits. For example, let's say a man past sixty tries to learn how to play football. It's foolish for him to do that, but only because his body is too old, not his mind!

2

Vocabulary

the local "tech": the technical college in a certain area. This is where adult education classes in languages and so on are held in the evenings.

permanent education: education that goes on throughout one's life without stopping at any fixed point.

limits: restrictions, points which cannot be passed.

3

Questions (to be answered after you have listened to the tape)

1 How did "the man in the street" feel about school when he was there?
2 How does the interviewer explain the idea of permanent education?
3 What does the man think about the idea?
4 The educational psychologist describes certain "limits"; what are they and why do they exist?
5 According to her, what happens as we get older?
6 What does she think we ought to do, and why?

Practice

4a

What are the correct prepositions?

1 When I was . . . . school, I hated it.
2 Some people go . . . . the local 'tech'.
3 As we get older we may not learn some things . . . . quickly . . . . before.

4b

Observe how two ideas are combined in this sentence on the tape.

He does that. It's foolish.
It's foolish for him to do that.

Now combine these ideas in the same way.

1 People go to evening classes. It's crazy.
2 They learn foreign languages. It's difficult.
3 Children smoke. It's bad.
4 That old man plays football. It's dangerous.
5 He plays golf. It's better.

5

Discussion (and/or extended writing)

1 Do you think we can be too old to learn certain things? What? Why?
2 What are the best and the worst memories you have of your own school days?
3 If you are over thirty, describe the differences between education *then* and education *now*.

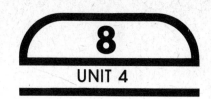
Margaret Dickinson is Wilson's secretary. She has decided to ask him for a rise.

1

Story

When Margaret went into Wilson's office, she noticed that he looked very tired. In fact, he looked awful. She knew it was not a good time to ask for a rise, but she felt she had to. She tried to think of something casual to say first. It was always best to begin such conversations casually.

"Uh . . . you're looking a bit tired," she said. Wilson sighed. He told her he had just seen the Financial Controller, the man who told everybody at the EBC how much they could spend.

"As usual, he said I was spending too much. It wasn't a very pleasant conversation," he said. Then he mentioned that he had a headache. Margaret began to feel sorry for him. She offered to get some aspirins for him from the canteen.

"You needn't bother. I can go there myself," he said.

"Oh, but I'm going to the canteen anyway. It's no trouble," she protested. Wilson thanked her and gave her some money for the aspirins. She left. It was only after she had closed the door behind her that she realised something. She had forgotten to ask for the rise!

2

Multiple Choice

1 Margaret asked for a rise. She wanted . . . .
(a) a higher position   (b) a bigger office
(c) more time to work   (d) more money
2 Wilson sighed. He . . . .
(a) made a sign with his hand   (b) made a noise
(c) looked sad   (d) looked angry
3 Margaret was going to the canteen *anyway*. She was going there . . . .
(a) in any case   (b) any possible way   (c) any possible time   (d) soon
4 *Bother* in *you needn't bother* means . . . .
(a) talk so much   (b) ask any more questions
(c) cause yourself trouble   (d) go immediately

3a

What do *you* say when someone else says things like, "I've got a terrible headache" or "My pet cat died today"? (Or do you just stare and say nothing?)

3b

Describe or explain:

1 why Margaret wanted to see Wilson
2 how he looked
3 what she tried to think of at first
4 what Wilson had just done
5 what sort of conversation he had had
6 why Margaret offered to get some aspirins for him
7 what Wilson said when she offered
8 what happened at the end

3c

Put the things Wilson says here into sentences with *told* or *said*.

"I'm very tired."
He *said* he *was* very tired.
"Margaret, I need an aspirin."
He *told* Margaret he *needed* an aspirin.

1 "I don't like the Controller."
2 "David, I like this work."
3 "I'll come later."
4 "Linda, it's getting late."
5 "It has been a terrible day."
6 "Margaret, the phone has just rung.'
7 "I'll answer it."
8 "David, it's important!"

3d

These things were expressed in single sentences. How?

1 She knew she should not ask for a rise. It was not a good time.
2 She wanted to say something casual first. She tried to think of it.

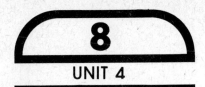

8

UNIT 4

Listen to the dialogue on tape. Then use this skeleton to reproduce what Wilson says.

1

Dialogue
Margaret has just come in
WILSON: .... morning, Margaret. .... this morning?
MARGARET: Oh, I'm all right, thank you. How are you?
WILSON: .... bad, ... thank you. Things ....
MARGARET: You're looking a bit tired.
WILSON: .... I?
MARGARET: Yes, you are.
WILSON: Well, ... the Financial Controller.
MARGARET: Oh, I see. And what happened?
WILSON: .... usual, he said .... spending too much. .... pleasant conversation.
MARGARET: Oh, I'm sorry to hear that.
WILSON: You .... aspirins on you .... any chance .... you?
MARGARET: Aspirins? No, I'm sorry. Why? Have you got a headache?
WILSON: Yes, ... afraid .... But .... matter.
MARGARET: They sell aspirins in the canteen, you know.
WILSON: Oh, ...?
MARGARET: Yes. I can get you some now. I'll go to the canteen now.
WILSON: .... very kind .... you, but .... bother .... some myself.
MARGARET: Oh, I'm going to the canteen anyway. It's no trouble.
WILSON: Well, ... case, if .... there anyway, perhaps .... a small packet.
MARGARET: Certainly. No trouble at all.
WILSON: .... very much, Margaret. Here's .... money.
MARGARET: Well, then, I'll bring them back after my coffee break, shall I?
WILSON: .... fine. Thanks ....
Margaret leaves the room
WILSON: Margaret! Margaret! (to himself) .... funny. She didn't .... why .... to see me.

Practice

2a

Wilson wants some aspirins. He asks Margaret:

"You haven't got any aspirins on you by any chance, have you?"

What does he ask her if he wants:
1 some money
2 some matches
3 a pencil
4 a cigarette
5 some pennies
6 a pen

2b

Margaret says:
"I'll go to the canteen now."
and Wilson answers:
"That's very kind of you, but you needn't bother. I can go there myself."

What are *his* answers if *she* says:
1 "I'll type that letter."
2 "I'll post those letters."
3 "I'll carry that bag for you."
4 "I'll take care of this matter."
5 "I'll solve the problem for you."
6 "I'll dial the number for you."

3

Transfer

Imagine the things people say just *before* you give these answers.
1 An old lady is telling you all her troubles. You keep saying, "I'm very sorry to hear that."
2 You are staying with a family in a foreign country. They keep offering to do things for you. But you are very tired and want to rest. You keep saying, "That's very kind of you but you needn't bother."

Grammar Summary/Revision

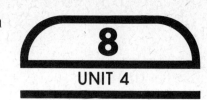

MODALS
Needn't/mustn't do

1a In the last three units we have studied various aspects of modals, such as the way they behave in reported speech, etc. Now examine this pair, which have important nuances in English.

> **1** MARGARET: **I'll go to the canteen and get those aspirins now.**
> ROBERT: **Oh, you needn't do that. I can wait until you come back from your coffee break.**
> **2** ROBERT: *(talking to Linda about the Financial Controller)*
> **He's always telling me I mustn't overspend.**

Comment **1b**

1 *Needn't do* means *it isn't necessary for you to do that.*
2 *Mustn't do* means *you shouldn't do that because it's not allowed.*

Practice **1c**

What do you say to the other person in these situations?
Use *needn't* or *mustn't.*
Example:

> SITUATION: **You are talking to a little girl. She is playing with some matches.**
> RESPONSE: **You *mustn't* play with those matches.**
> SITUATION: **Someone is speaking English to you very slowly.**
> RESPONSE: **You *needn't* speak so slowly.**

1 You are in a petrol station. Someone is smoking.
2 You are in someone's house. They are going to turn the heating up. You are warm enough.
3 Your secretary is willing to work late. You can do the work without her.
4 Your friend is going to park his car where there is a sign saying, "No Parking".

5 Your friend is willing to drive you somewhere. You are willing to walk.
6 Your friend is going out and it is going to rain. You can see he is going to forget his umbrella.
7 Someone is shouting at you but you are not deaf.
8 Your taxi driver is willing to wait but it is not necessary.

EXTENDED WRITING
(and/or oral practice)

2a Write a dialogue for this situation.

1 Margaret Dickinson has an interview with her boss, Robert Wilson. She wants a rise but does not say so at first.
2 She is looking tired. Wilson asks her why.
3 She says that her mother (who is old and lives with her) has been very ill and that she, Margaret, has been looking after her.
4 Wilson offers to give her a few days off. Margaret says it isn't necessary.

5 She finally gets to the point. She asks for the rise. Wilson says he would like to give her a rise but the Financial Controller would be against it.
6 Margaret says politely but firmly that if she does not get a rise she will have to find another job.
7 Wilson says he will talk to the Financial Controller, promises to do all he can, and to let her know by the end of the week.

2b Do the discussion questions on page 36 in writing.

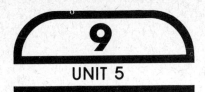

THE RICH AND THE POOR

1

The world is divided into two main parts. The difference is that one part is rich and the other is poor. In the poor part, a lot of people never get enough to eat. In the rich part a lot of people eat too much. In one part, children starve and in the other, a lot of people get fatter and fatter and have to go on diets, or do special exercises in order to lose weight.

Questions

You are interviewing an expert on world problems. Get him to tell you about:

1 the difference between the two main parts of the world
2 the number of people who don't get enough to eat and where they are
3 children in the poor part
4 the things that happen in the rich part

Imagine his answers as well.

2

The poorer countries are called "the developing countries". They have special problems. Sometimes the land is too poor to grow anything on. The land can be improved but a lot of things must be done first. New farming methods must be introduced. The people must be educated. Water must be found.

Many of these problems are too big for one country to solve alone. Help should be given by the richer countries but it must be the right sort of help. Money is not enough. The developing countries must be helped to help themselves.

Questions

Continue the interview. Get the expert to tell you about:

1 the special problems of the developing countries
2 what can be done
3 what must be done first
4 why he thinks help should be given
5 who should give the help
6 what sort of help
7 why money is not enough

Imagine the expert's answers as well.

3

But rich countries have problems, too. They are not always very pleasant places to live in. Usually, it is the things that make them rich that also make them unpleasant.

Sometimes the air is too filthy to breathe and the rivers are too filthy to swim in or to take water from. Perhaps almost everybody has a car but the roads are too crowded to drive along. And sometimes, even in these countries, large numbers of people do not have decent houses to live in.

Something will have to be done about these problems, too. The air and the rivers will have to be cleaned, and more houses will have to be built.

Questions

a
Ask the expert questions about the "rich" countries. The questions must *end in these words*.

1 pleasant places to live in?
2 pleasant to breathe?
3 nice to swim in?
4 good places to take water from?
5 pleasant to drive along?
6 all the houses decent places to live in?
7 done about these problems?

b
You are the leader of a team of architects and engineers. You want to improve a typical industrial area. Tell a reporter what will have to be done and why. Talk about:

1 the rivers
2 the air
3 the roads
4 some of the houses, etc.

Discussion

Think of such an industrial area that you know yourself or have read about. What are the advantages and disadvantages of living in it when compared with a poorer but more pleasant part of the world?

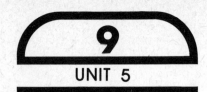

UNIT 5

The land can be improved.

1

A government official is putting questions to an expert on world problems. Respond as the expert does.

> OFFICIAL: **Can you improve this land?**
> EXPERT: **Yes, the land can be improved.**
>
> OFFICIAL: **Should we give help?**
> EXPERT: **Yes, help should be given.**

1 Can you solve this problem?
2 Must we do something now?
3 Can you find water?
4 Must we spend a lot of money?
5 Should we buy tractors?
6 Can you train these people?
7 Can we grow food here?
8 Will we have to buy new machines?
9 Will we have to build roads?
10 Ought we to start the work now?

The land is too poor to farm. The people are too poor to farm it.

2a

Combine these pairs, like this.

> **The land is too poor. It can't be farmed.**
> **The land is too poor to farm.**
>
> **The people are too poor. They can't farm it.**
> **The people are too poor to farm the land.**

1 The people are too weak. They can't work.
2 This job is too difficult. It can't be done.
3 I'm too busy. I can't go out.
4 This tractor is too old. It can't be repaired.
5 This tractor is too small. It can't do the job.
6 Some people are too old. They can't change.
7 This problem is too difficult. It can't be explained.
8 You're too young. You can't understand this.

2b

Comment

Notice that the same active infinitive form (*to farm*) is used in the example to express both:

It can't be farmed. (passive) and
They can't farm it. (active)

2c

Transfer

You are a student at a Language Institute and you are talking to a teacher. Make excuses for all the things you did not do last week, like: "*The homework was too .... to ....*" and "*I was too .... to ....*" etc.

The land is too poor to grow anything on.

3

Two students are talking. Respond as B does. Notice the position of the preposition at the end of the sentence.

A: **Why didn't you listen to the lecture? Was it too boring?**
B: **Yes, exactly. It was too boring to listen to.**

1 Was the lecture too long? Is that why you didn't sit through it?
2 Why didn't you go to that talk? Was it too late?
3 Why didn't you sit in that room? Was it too crowded?
4 Why didn't you sit on the floor? Was it too hard?
5 Was the lecture too early? Is that why you didn't go to it?
6 Why didn't you talk to the professor? Was he too far away?

The problem is too big for one country to solve.

4a

A man and his wife are arguing. Respond as B does.

A: **This bag is very heavy. Here, *you* carry it.**
B: **No! It's too heavy for me to carry.**

1 This is a good steak. I think the dog should eat it.
2 What a terrible film! Let the children watch it.
3 This bed is very dirty. I think the children should sleep in it.
4 This chair is very hard. Why don't you sit in it?
5 This is a very good sweater. I think my mother should have it.
6 This sweater is very old. Here. *You* wear it.

4b

Transfer

You are looking at a small house in England for you and your family of four. The owner of the house is showing you the rooms. There is always something wrong. For example:

OWNER: **This is the dining room.**
YOU: **Hmm. It's very small, isn't it? I mean, it's too small for four people to eat in.**

What do you say when the owner shows you:

1 a small bedroom for you and your wife
2 a cold bedroom for a young child
3 a small study for you to work in
4 a small kitchen
5 an old cooker
6 a very small garage (you have a large car)
7 very hard chairs
8 a small, dark garden (your children would want to play in it)

Think of other things that might be wrong with the house and what you would say about them.

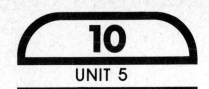

An economist talks about the problems of the poorer countries.

1

Text

It isn't strictly true that one half of the world is rich and the other half is poor. It is one-third that is very rich and two-thirds that are very poor. People in the rich third don't realise the enormous difference between them and the other two-thirds. A very simple example is that a dog or a cat in North America eats better than a child in the poorer countries. A fisherman in South America may be catching fish which is processed into pet food and yet his own children are not getting enough protein for their bodies to develop properly. Although a lot of the world's natural resources like oil come from these poorer countries, we in the richer countries are probably using sixty times as much of these resources as a person in Asia or Africa. The richer countries are in a position to dictate to suppliers what kind of prices they are prepared to pay for these natural resources. In some cases the prices have gone down. In others they have remained steady. But the prices the richer countries get for their own exports have continued to rise. So they are getting richer and richer and the poorer countries are getting poorer.

2

Vocabulary

strictly true: exactly true.

protein: the things in food that build up the body and are necessary for good health.

processed into pet food: made into food for dogs, cats and other pets.

develop properly: develop as they should.

natural resources: basic materials like oil, natural gas, and the things needed to make iron, steel, etc.

using up: using all of something.

suppliers: (here) the poorer countries that supply or produce natural resources.

remain steady: stay the same.

3

Questions (to be answered after you have listened to the tape)

1 What is the mistake the interviewer makes at the beginning?
2 What are the "two divisions" the economist speaks about and what does he say about them?
3 What happens to the fish a South American fisherman catches, and what is strange about this?
4 Why is the interviewer surprised when he hears that the richer countries are using up the world's natural resources?
5 What is one reason for the fact that the richer countries are getting richer and the poorer countries are getting poorer?

4

Practice

Observe how these two ideas are expressed in one sentence.

> **Children don't get enough protein. Their bodies don't develop properly.**
> **Children don't get enough protein for their bodies to develop properly.**

Combine these ideas in the same way.

1 There isn't enough time. The man can't do this job.
2 He doesn't speak clearly enough. The students can't understand.
3 This train doesn't leave early enough. We can't reach London before 5.
4 It doesn't rain enough. The plants don't grow properly.

5

Discussion (and/or extended writing)

What other arguments have you heard for and against giving help to poorer countries? Describe the arguments. Then say what you think of them.

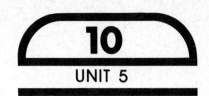

Linda recently went to Liverpool by train.

1

Story

Linda found a seat in a compartment that was full of middle-aged businessmen. One of them offered to put her case on the rack for her. She politely told him she could do it herself. The man started talking to her after she had sat down. She tried to avoid getting into a conversation but it was impossible. He was one of those boring types that go on talking even if nobody is interested.

When she casually mentioned that she was going to Liverpool in order to do a report on the city, he began telling her all about the place. Several hours went by. He talked and talked. Linda hardly said anything. Finally, the train got into Liverpool. The man kept on talking until the very last minute. Linda got up to go. Just then he invited her to a party. He said he would introduce her to all his friends so that she could learn more about Liverpool. Linda politely refused and hurried out of the compartment. She could still hear the man's voice. He was talking to someone else in the compartment and she happened to catch a few words.

"Nice girl," he was saying. "But you know, she talked so much that I could hardly get a word in edgeways."

2

Vocabulary

Find the words or phrases in the text that mean these things.

1 a part of a train where people sit
2 where you put your suitcase
3 say something in a casual way
4 arrive in
5 ask someone to come to a party, etc
6 say 'no'
7 leave quickly
8 I could hardly say anything myself

3

Questions

1 Who else was in the compartment?
2 What did the man do when Linda came in?

3 What did Linda try to avoid? Why?
4 Why was she going to Liverpool?
5 What happened when she mentioned this?
6 What happened during the journey?
7 What happened just after the train got into Liverpool?

Practice

4a

▌ She tried to *avoid getting* into a conversation.

What did she try to avoid if she did not want to:

1 miss the train
2 be impolite
3 look bored
4 get into an argument
5 sit next to the man in the dining car
6 give the impression she liked the man

4b

Transfer

Yesterday you were driving through town when your brakes suddenly failed. What did you try to avoid doing? You almost:

1 ran into a lorry
2 hit an old lady
3 knocked down some children
4 wrecked the car
5 got killed

Think of other examples.

4c

▌ The man was *boring*. Linda was *bored*.

What can we say about both the man and Linda if he was the sort who:

1 amuses people
2 interests them
3 disgusts them
4 irritates them
5 frightens them
6 annoys them

4d

How were these ideas expressed in single sentences?

1 She was going to Liverpool. She was going to do a report.
2 She got up. She wanted to go.
3 He would introduce her to his friends. She could learn more about Liverpool.

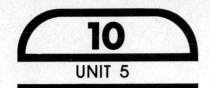

Dialogue/Practice

10
UNIT 5

Listen to the dialogue on tape. Then use this skeleton to reproduce what Linda says.

1

Dialogue
Linda has just got on the train to Liverpool
LINDA: .... this seat ....?
MAN: No. No, it isn't.
LINDA: ....
MAN: Let me help you with your case.
LINDA: No, ... right. .... manage, ... kind, ... same.
MAN: Well, you got here just in time, didn't you? The train seems to be leaving now.
LINDA: .... lucky.
MAN: Going to Liverpool, are you?
LINDA: .... right.
MAN: Got friends there, have you?
LINDA: No, ... business, ...
MAN: On business? Really?
LINDA: .... happen .... the time?
MAN: Yes, it's a quarter past 10. What sort of business?
LINDA: .... a reporter. I'm .... Liverpool .... a report on it.
MAN: Really! So you're a reporter. Now, I know a lot about Liverpool!
LINDA: ....? .... interesting.
MAN: Let me tell you about it.
The man goes on talking. Several hours later the train arrives in Liverpool. The man has been talking all the time.
LINDA: .... goodbye. I .... go now.
MAN: Just a moment. I'm giving a party this evening. Why don't you come?
LINDA: Well, ... like ...., but I'm afraid ....
MAN: I'll introduce you to all my friends so that you can learn more about Liverpool.
LINDA: No, ..., I'm .... won't be able ....
MAN (*after Linda has left*): Nice girl, but you know, when we talked I could hardly get a word in edgeways.

Practice

2a

The man offers to help Linda with her case. He says:

▌ **"Let me help you with your case."**

What does he say if he offers to:
1   carry her suitcase
2   give her some help
3   tell her about Liverpool
4   take her to a party
5   show her around Liverpool

2b

The man thinks the train is leaving, but he is not absolutely sure. He says:

▌ **"The train seems to be leaving now."**

What does he say if he thinks:
1   the train is running late
2   it is waiting for something
3   the other passengers are getting angry
4   they are arguing with the conductor
5   all the trains are running late

2c

The man asks Linda if she is going to Liverpool. He is sure the answer is *yes*. He says:

▌ **"Going to Liverpool, are you?"**

In the same way, ask Linda if she:
1   has been to Liverpool before
2   is going there on business
3   is working for the EBC
4   has just got on the train
5   is visiting Manchester, too
6   is doing a report on Liverpool

3

Transfer
A young Englishman is travelling by train in your country. You can see he has just come from England, is going to the capital, etc. Think of things to say to begin a conversation.

Grammar Summary/Revision

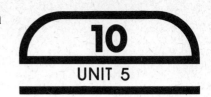

INFINITIVE PARTICLES   **1**   After verbs like *want, like, expect, hope*, etc., which can be followed by a full infinitive (*to do*) we often leave out the verb if *it is already understood*. This happens often in spoken English. For example:

A: **Do you hope to find a better job?**
B: **Yes, I hope to, but I don't know if I will.**

Now answer as B did with, "Yes, I hope/want/etc. to, but . . ."

1 Would you like to go to the party?
2 Do you want to buy that car?
3 Will you pass the exam?
4 I understand you intend to get a better job?
5 Is it true you have to work on Sunday?
6 You know, you ought to ask your boss for a rise!
7 Do you hope to get a rise?

PRESENT CONTINUOUS (future use)   Comment **2a**   **I'm giving a party this evening.**

This *future* use of the present continuous suggests that plans or arrangements have already been made for something to happen. For example, the man who says this had probably already invited guests, ordered some wine, etc.

2b   Now suppose *you are on a plane at the moment between London and New York*. Make examples of your own about yourself like this. Before you left London you arranged to meet a friend in Times Square this evening.

"I'm meeting a friend in Times Square this evening."

1 You also arranged to have dinner at Jack's bar on 34th Street this evening.
2 On the phone your friend said, "Let's go to the theatre this evening." You agreed.
3 You also arranged to stay at the George Washington Hotel.
4 On the phone your friend said, "Let's watch a football game." You agreed.
5 You also arranged to leave New York on Friday.

EXTENDED WRITING (and/or oral practice)   **3**   Write a conversation for the following situation.

Linda gets on a train to Manchester. A young man helps her with two heavy suitcases. He starts a conversation with her. She is interested in him but tries not to show it at first. He asks her why she is going to Manchester and about her job. He tells her he is an architect. He invites her out for dinner that evening. She is happy to accept. He tells her he will call for her, asks her where she is staying so that he can come for her, and before they arrive in Manchester, they both become very friendly with each other.

HOLIDAYS

1

"Package holidays" are becoming more and more popular. That is the sort of holiday these people are going on. A travel agency has chartered the plane they are going to travel in, reserved the hotel they will stay at and even ordered the food they will eat. That is why it is called a package holiday. Such holidays are usually rather cheap. That is probably why they are so popular. But not everybody likes them. Some people say you do not see very much of the country you go to.

Questions

You are interviewing the owner of a travel agency. Ask him:

1 if such holidays are becoming more popular
2 why
3 what the travel agency has done for these people
4 if such holidays are very expensive
5 if everybody likes them
6 why not

Give his answers as well.

2

These young people are going abroad, too. But they are not going on a package holiday. And their holiday will not be very expensive, either. They will probably walk most of the way. Sometimes they will get "lifts" in lorries or cars. They will stay in youth hostels. Sometimes they will even sleep in parks or fields. That is how a lot of young people see the world these days.

Questions

Now imagine you are interviewing some of these young people. Ask:

1 if they are going on a package holiday
2 where they are going
3 if their holiday will be very expensive
4 how they will travel
5 where they will stay

Discussion

Give reasons for recommending one sort of holiday or the other to:

1 your aunt Agatha, who is fifty-five and unmarried. She wants to go abroad but does not like foreigners or foreign food
2 a student with no money
3 a man and his wife with a family of three and not too much money

3

It is getting easier and easier to travel but it is getting harder and harder to get away from other people. Perhaps that is the most difficult thing of all.

These people thought a camping holiday would be a good idea. But they were not able to find a camping site they really liked. They managed to find an empty place in the forest only after they had spent hours looking. The police will probably come in a few minutes and tell them they cannot camp anywhere they like. They will probably have to go to a crowded camping site somewhere.

Questions

Interview these people. Ask them:
1 why they went on a camping holiday
2 if it was easy to find a camping site
3 how long it took them to find an empty place in the forest
4 if the police will come soon
5 what the police will tell them
6 where they will have to go

4

This is the Griffin family. The holiday they have decided on is a winter holiday and the place they are going to is a winter resort in the Alps.

It is almost the end of the winter season. They are going now because there is still a lot of snow but the mountains are less crowded. They hope to do a lot of skiing and, at the same time, avoid huge crowds of people and very high prices. Even then, such a holiday is far from cheap. They managed to save up for it by cutting down on luxuries.

Questions

Interview the Griffins. Ask them:
1 what sort of holiday they are going on
2 where they are going
3 why they are going at the end of the season
4 what they hope to do
5 if such a holiday is cheap
6 how they managed to save up for it

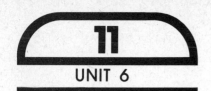

Grammar Exposition and Exercises

That's the sort of holiday
these people are going on.

1

Two students are talking. Respond as B does.
Notice the position of the preposition at the end
of his response.

> A: **Are you really going to stay at the Hilton Hotel?**
> B: **Yes, that's right. That's the hotel I'm going to stay at.**

1 Are you really going to travel in that huge plane?
2 And are you really going to travel with that beautiful girl?
3 So you're really going on this "millionaire's holiday"?
4 And you're really going to sleep in that golden bed?
5 Are you really going to swim in that huge pool?
6 And you're going to dance with that beautiful blonde?
7 Are you really going to work for that big company?
8 And you're going to sit behind that big desk?

That's where/how/why . . .

2a

A stranger is trying to impress you. You are trying
to impress him.

> STRANGER: **I always travel in the best trains.**
> YOU: **That's how I travel, too.**
> STRANGER: **I travel in them because they're so much faster.**
> YOU: **That's why I travel in them, too.**
> STRANGER: **I always stay at the best hotel in town.**
> YOU: **That's where I stay, too.**

1 I always travel first class.
2 I always sit in the best seat.
3 I sit there because it's more comfortable.
4 I live in the best part of town, you know.
5 I live there because you meet such nice people there.
6 I buy my clothes from the best shop.
7 I buy them there because the service is much better.
8 I earn my living as a comedian, you know.

2b

Transfer

Now carry on the conversation. Talk about the
restaurants you eat at, why you eat there, where
you spend your holidays, why, etc.

It's getting harder and
harder . . .

3

You are lying on a crowded beach with a friend.
Respond as B does. Remember that one- or two-
syllable adjectives form the comparative like *hard*
(*hard/harder*). Adjectives of more than two syl-
lables are like *difficult* (*difficult/more difficult*).

> A: **The beach is very crowded now.**
> B: **Yes, and it's getting more crowded.**
> A: **The wind is very strong.**
> B: **Yes, and it's getting stronger.**

1 The sun's hot.
2 Those children are noisy.
3 Look how dark the sky is!
4 The weather's rather unpleasant now.
5 Cold this morning, isn't it?
6 It's difficult to find an empty beach.

**The most difficult thing
of all . . .**

**They managed to find an
empty place in the forest.**

4a

You are still on the beach. Respond as B does.
Remember that one- or two-syllable adjectives form
the superlative like *hard (hard/the hardest)*. Others
are like *difficult (difficult/the most difficult)*.

> A: **It's difficult to find an empty beach.**
> B: **Yes, that's the most difficult thing of all.**
> A: **It's nice to lie in the sun.**
> B: **Yes, that's the nicest thing of all.**

1 It's hard to find an empty beach.
2 It's pleasant to lie on an empty one.
3 It's very tiring to look for one.
4 It's very boring, too.
5 But it's wonderful to lie in the sun.
6 And it's cheap, too.

4b

Transfer

Imagine a similar conversation between two motorists. Say how difficult it is to find a parking space,
how expensive it is to run a car these days, how hard
it is to find good mechanics, etc.

5a

Managed to . . . indicates that something was difficult to do but that you did it. Imagine you are
talking about your holiday. You managed to do a
lot of difficult things. For example:

> Situation: **The sun did not shine very much but
> you got a good suntan.**
> You say: **I managed to get a good suntan even
> though the sun didn't shine very much.**

Now find some more responses for these situations.

1 The town was full of tourists but you found a
   good, cheap hotel.
2 The beach was very crowded but you found an
   empty spot.
3 You have very little money but you had a very
   good time.
4 There wasn't very much snow but you did a lot
   of skiing.
5 It was very noisy but you went to sleep.
6 You had never learned the language before but
   you understood almost everything.

5b

Transfer

You had to travel to London suddenly a few days
ago. Think of all the things you managed to do. For
example:

1 you got on the midnight train
2 you had three heavy bags
3 the train was very crowded
4 you arrived very late and you were hungry, etc.

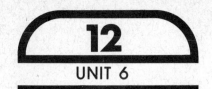

Intensive Listening

12
UNIT 6

The Griffin Family (see text 4, page 49) talk about their holiday.

1

Text (shortened and adapted) of Mr and Mrs Griffin's remarks and comments.

We were beginning to get more and more fed up with the "holiday by the sea". We always used to go to the south coast regularly for a fortnight every summer. There wasn't a chance to have a proper summer holiday last year, so we decided we'd better have some sort of a winter holiday. Some friends of ours had told us we might not enjoy a skiing holiday, that it was always so cold you had to go skiing just to keep warm. We only had eight days instead of our normal fortnight away. All together, with the return flight, accommodation, etc., it came to about £125 for the three of us. And it was worth every penny. I mean, I work hard all the year round. I need a complete change and I'm willing to pay for it. I'd certainly recommend a holiday like this to anyone. We saved up for it, by the way, by cutting down on luxuries.

2

Vocabulary

fed up with: frustrated and irritated with.

fortnight: British English expression for two weeks.

accommodation: where you stay.

cut down on: consume less of or use less of. Example: "You'd better cut down on smoking."

3

Questions (to be answered after you have listened to the tape)

1 What have the Griffins just done?
2 Where did they use to spend their holidays?
3 How were they beginning to feel about this?
4 What happened to Mr Griffin last spring?
5 Why didn't he have a "proper" summer holiday?
6 How did Mrs Griffin feel about the idea of a winter holiday at first?
7 Why did she feel this way?
8 How much did it cost all together and what did this include?

9 Why does Mr Griffin feel it was "worth every penny"?
10 How did they manage to save up for it?

 Practice

4a

Listen to the tape again carefully and listen to the way the following words or phrases are used. Then make sentences of your own using these same words in the same way:

1 keen   4 eventually
2 to start with   5 suggested
3 at first   6 recommend

4b

Supply the missing words.

1 Did you enjoy the holiday .... much .... you thought you .... ?
2 There wasn't a chance .... a proper summer holiday .... we decided .... some sort .... winter holiday.
3 I wasn't terribly keen .... the idea .... first.
4 We didn't spent quite .... much .... usual .... Christmas.

5

Discussion (and/or extended writing)

Describe your idea of a terrible holiday!
What is your idea of a good one?
What in your opinion are the worst things about "package holidays"?
What are the good things about them?

Story/Dialogue

Robert Wilson is going to the Swiss Alps for a holiday. He is going to fly there.

1

Story

When Wilson got to the airport, his flight was already being called over the loudspeakers. The day before he had cancelled his ticket for a morning flight and had booked an afternoon flight instead. He had to go to the reservations desk to collect his new ticket.

He apologised for being late. The reservations clerk smiled and began to look through the reservations in front of her. Then her smile disappeared and she began to look worried.

"Your ticket doesn't seem to be here," she said. "Let me check it with the computer."

The computer clicked and whirred and lights began to flash. Just then, his flight was called a second time. Wilson became very nervous. Finally the girl looked up.

"There's been a mistake. Your new ticket was sent to you by post. That's why it isn't here," she said. It took her only a short time to write out a new one. Wilson managed to catch the plane just before it took off. "What a way to start a holiday," he thought.

2

Vocabulary

Find the words that mean these things.

1   He had *informed the airport that he did not need the ticket*.
2   He had *to get* the ticket.
3   It *made mechanical noises*.
4   Lights began *to go on and off*.
5   The plane *left the ground*.
6   He was able *to get on the plane in time*.

3

Questions

1   What was happening when Wilson got to the airport?
2   What had he done the day before?
3   Why did the clerk begin to look worried?
4   What happened then?
5   Why wasn't Wilson's ticket there?
6   What happened at the end?

Practice

4a

What are the missing words?

Wilson had . . . . his ticket . . . . a morning . . . . the day . . . . and had . . . . an afternoon . . . . The reservations . . . . began to . . . . the . . . . in . . . . of . . . . . She could not find it, so she . . . . it . . . . the computer. She found that his . . . . had been . . . . to him . . . . post.

4b

■   **Wilson apologised for being late.**

What did he apologise for if he:

1   forgot his ticket
2   came late
3   disturbed the clerk
4   caused her a lot of trouble
5   made a lot of other people late
6   kept the plane waiting

4c

■   **It took her only a short time to write out a new one.**

Express these ideas the same way.

1   She did it in five minutes.
2   He got there in an hour.
3   We learned this after a long time.
4   They understood this after only a short time.
5   I got dressed in only a few minutes.

5

Transfer

Say how long it took you to:

1   get to school or to work this morning
2   read this page
3   do these exercises

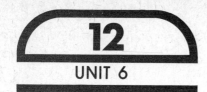

12

UNIT 6

Listen to the dialogue on tape. Then use this skeleton to reproduce what Wilson says.

1

Dialogue
Wilson has just arrived at the airport.
His flight is being called when he arrives
CLERK: Good afternoon, sir. Can I help you?
WILSON: Yes, ... I've come .... ticket ....
   2 o'clock flight .... Zurich. That's the one ....
   called. My name ....
CLERK: Just let me look through these reservations
   here. Yours should be among them.
WILSON: My secretary .... reservation .... phone.
CLERK: I see. Uh huh.
WILSON: .... sorry .... earlier .... so much
   traffic! And .... some work to do .... my office
   this morning.
CLERK: Hmm. That's strange!
WILSON: .... wrong?
CLERK: It's your reservation, sir. It doesn't seem to
   be here.
WILSON: But .... impossible! .... some mistake.
CLERK: Just let me check it with the computer.
The computer clicks and whirs
WILSON: .... long? .... catch it!
CLERK: Yes, sir. Just a moment, sir. It's all right,
   sir. There's been a mistake. Your new ticket was
   sent to you by post. That's why it isn't here.
Wilson's name is called
WILSON: .... me! .... me now!
CLERK: Don't worry! It'll only take me a minute to
   write out a new ticket!
WILSON: .... hold the flight .... me?
CLERK: That won't be necessary. Just take your
   luggage to the Last-Minute Check-In. They
   reserve it for passengers in a hurry.
WILSON: .... my new ticket yet!
CLERK: That's all right. I'll bring it over myself.
   Hurry, or you'll miss the plane, sir!

Practice

2a

The clerk *supposes* that Wilson's reservation is among the others.

■ **"Yours should be among them."**

Transform in the same way.
1 The reservation is in the post.
2 The other clerk knows where it is.
3 It is in the office somewhere.
4 The other clerk has it.
5 It's in the office upstairs.

2b

Wilson is late. He *apologises*.

■ **"I'm sorry I wasn't able to come earlier."**

How would he apologise if it was impossible to:
1 inform the airline sooner
2 phone sooner
3 leave work earlier
4 check in on time

2c

Transfer
Your best friend got married yesterday. Apologise
because you did not:
1 send any flowers
2 get to the party
3 give a present
Think of other things you did not do and apologise
for them in the same way.

2d

The clerk thinks Wilson's ticket *is not there*. She says:

■ **"Your ticket does not seem to be here."**

What does she say to Wilson if she thinks:
1 he does not understand
2 there is not a ticket in his name
3 his name is not on any of the tickets
4 his plane does not leave from London
5 the other clerk does not know about it.

Grammar Summary/Revision

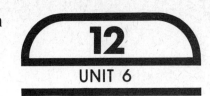

RELATIVE PRONOUNS   **1a**   Observe where a relative pronoun is necessary and where it is not.

Kernels

1 These are people. They have arranged a package holiday through a travel agency.
2 It is still possible to have a holiday. It is both pleasant and reasonably cheap.
3 A travel agency has even ordered the food. They will eat it.
4 A travel agency has booked the hotel. They are going to stay at it.

Results

1 These are people who have arranged a package holiday through a travel agency.
2 It is still possible to have a holiday that is both pleasant and reasonably cheap.
3 A travel agency has even ordered the food they will eat.
4 A travel agency has booked the hotel they are going to stay at.

Comments **1b**   (These tell you things you may already know, but read them carefully.)

1 *Who* is the relative pronoun used for people. *Which* is used for things.
2 *That* may be used for both people and things.
3 A relative pronoun is *not* necessary when it is the *object*, and *not* the *subject* of the second clause.
4 Note the position of the preposition *at* in 4. Prepositions such as these (which refer to a relative pronoun) normally occur in this position in the spoken language.

Practice **1c**   Now produce "result sentences" from these "kernels".

1 They're people. They're staying here.
2 That's the house. I'm living in it.
3 I know a family. They've just gone away.
4 That's the family. I spoke about them.
5 What's that book? You're reading it.

6 Who's that girl? You're staring at her.
7 Who's that girl? She's just left.
8 What's that thing? It's fallen down.
9 Where's that book? It was here a moment ago.

EXTENDED WRITING   **2**   Write a conversation or a page from a novel for this situation.
(and/or oral practice)

1 Robert Wilson arrives at a hotel late at night. His secretary has booked a room for him there.
2 He apologises for arriving so late (his plane was delayed).
3 The hotel clerk smiles and looks through the guest list (the list of people who are staying at the hotel or who have reserved rooms).
4 The clerk begins to look worried, says that Wilson's name is not on the list and that there are no rooms free that evening.

5 Wilson is sure the clerk is wrong about this.
6 The clerk checks the guest list again and suddenly notices that there is a room reserved for "R. Wilton". The clerk says that someone has spelt Wilson's name wrongly and apologises. The clerk calls a porter who takes Wilson's luggage to his room.

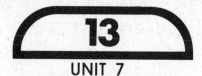
DISASTER

1

One night in April 1912, a huge new ocean liner was crossing the Atlantic. She was carrying 2,000 passengers. She was also going very fast, which was dangerous because there were icebergs around. The passengers were all having a good time when the ship suddenly struck one of these icebergs.

The ship began to sink and the passengers tried to escape, but there were not enough lifeboats. Another ship was passing nearby. The *Titanic* fired rockets into the air in order to get the other ship's help. It could have saved most of the passengers, but it did not even stop. Two thirds of the passengers went down with the *Titanic*. It was one of the greatest sea disasters of all time.

Questions

a

Find questions and answers. You are interviewing a writer who has written a book about the *Titanic* disaster. You want to know:

1 when the disaster happened
2 what sort of ship the *Titanic* was
3 how many passengers she was carrying
4 what caused the disaster
5 what the passengers were doing when the ship struck the iceberg
6 what they all tried to do
7 if there were enough lifeboats
8 if any other ships were passing
9 what the *Titanic* did to get help
10 if the other ship stopped
11 if it could have helped
12 how many passengers went down with the *Titanic*

b

Now imagine you are interviewing a very old lady who was a very young girl at the time and was actually on the *Titanic*. Think of all the questions you might want to ask and the answers she might give. For example, you could ask what she was doing when the disaster happened, how she got away, what the other passengers were doing when the ship finally went down, etc.

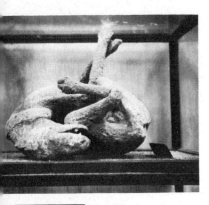

2

Some disasters can be avoided. Others cannot. Pompeii was a town near Naples, in Italy. It was also near a volcano. Suddenly, almost 2,000 years ago, the volcano erupted. This dog was trying to run away when it was buried alive. Hot ashes and stone covered everything in a few minutes.

Pompeii was recently dug out of the ashes. Many of the people who died were as well-preserved as this dog. When we look at them now, we can imagine almost exactly what they were doing when the volcano suddenly erupted.

Questions

a

1 What was Pompeii, where was it, and what happened there?

2 What was the dog doing when it was buried alive?

3 Is this the only thing that was found in the ashes?

4 What can we imagine when we look at the other things dug out of the ashes?

b

Now imagine what the following people were doing when the volcano erupted.

1 a baker

2 a farmer

3 a fisherman

4 a young mother with four children

5 the tax collector

6 a vegetable-seller in the market place

c

What do you think all these people did when the volcano erupted?

3

This was once a city. Here, the question is not, "What caused the disaster?" but "Who caused it?"

The city was destroyed by men. They knew exactly what they were doing. This type of disaster is called "War".

Can wars be avoided? Could the destruction of this city have been avoided? Perhaps not, but if the answer is "No", we can ask another question. Can the end of mankind be avoided?

Questions

Find questions for these answers, like this.

Answer: It was once a city.
You ask: What was this once?

1 Men did.

2 Yes, they knew exactly what they were doing.

3 It's called "War".

4 I don't know if they can be.

5 Yes, perhaps it could have been.

6 I hope it can be.

13

UNIT 7

The passengers were having a good time when the ship struck an iceberg.

1a

Comment

The past continuous is used here for something *that had started before and was still going on when something else happened.*

1b

All these things must have happened to you at one time or the other. Say what *you were doing at the time.* For example:

Situation: **You suddenly fell down.**
You say: **I was walking down the road** or **I was climbing a tree when I suddenly fell down.**

1 It started to rain.
2 The waiter said "May I have your order now?"
3 The alarm went off.
4 A dog began to bark at you.
5 Your teacher or boss came in and shouted, "What's going on here?"
6 You began to feel very cold.

1c

Now describe *what you did* when these things happened.

The other ship could have saved most of the passengers.

2

Could have . . . is used here to indicate that something *was possible in the past but never happened.* Respond as B does. Imagine you are talking to someone who has written a book on the *Titanic* disaster.

A: **The other ship didn't help. It just sailed away.**
B: **In other words, the other ship could have helped but it didn't.**

1 Some passengers didn't escape even though there was some room in the lifeboats.
2 They didn't even get into the boats.
3 The telegraph operator knew there were icebergs around. He didn't tell the captain.
4 The *Titanic* didn't avoid the iceberg even though it saw it in good time.
5 For some reason, the other ship didn't stop.
6 And so, all those people were never saved.

3

Transfer

Imagine you are an old man or woman. You are looking back at all the things you never did when you were younger. You are sure you could have done all these things.

Example: **You never became rich.**
You say: **I could have become rich, but I didn't. What a pity.**

Think of more things you might say. For example: you never learned Chinese, became a famous film star, travelled round the world, etc.

The _Titanic_ was going very fast, which was dangerous.

4

Which is used here to refer to the whole first part of the sentence. Use it the same way to make these pairs into single sentences.

1 She was not carrying enough lifeboats. This was very foolish.
2 The other ship did not stop. This surprised everybody.
3 Everybody was having a good time. This was only normal.
4 Some people gave their places in the lifeboats to other people. This was brave.
5 A lot of other people fought wildly to get into the boats. This is understandable.
6 The _Titanic_ went down and over a thousand lives were lost. This shocked the world.

What sank the _Titanic_?
What did the _Titanic_ strike?

5a

Remember again that when _what_ or _who_ is the _subject_ of the sentence, we do _not_ use _do/does_ or _did_ in the question. Now imagine you are asking the writer of the book on the _Titanic_ more questions. What do you ask if you know that:

1 something (but you don't know what) caused the disaster
2 someone knew about the icebergs
3 the _Titanic_ hit something
4 it fired something into the air
5 someone on the other ship saw the rockets
6 someone told the captain about it
7 he said something to one of the sailors
8 someone screamed
9 something happened to the _Titanic_ then
10 the passengers did something then
11 someone escaped with five suitcases

5b

Transfer

Situation: You have just found out that your friend had a fight with someone last night. You want to know more about what happened. You ask questions like, "Who did you have a fight with?"

Think of more questions. Think of the answers, too. For example, you know that:

1 someone gave him a black eye
2 he knocked someone out
3 someone called the police
4 he did something when they came
5 someone arrested him
6 he slept with someone in gaol
7 someone gave him breakfast, etc.

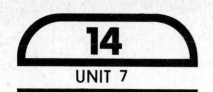

Intensive Listening

Important Note: From this point onwards the *Intensive Listening* does not contain a shortened and adapted text. In other words, it becomes a real test of *listening* comprehension.

 This is an interview with an author who has written a book about the *Titanic*.

1

Vocabulary

maiden voyage: the first voyage of a new ship.

luxurious: full of luxury, very comfortable and magnificent.

floating: anything that will stay on the water without sinking floats.

icebergs: huge mountains of ice that float in the Atlantic.

a slight mist: a very thin kind of fog.

SOS signal: signal sent out when a ship is in trouble and needs help.

wake (woke/woken): to get up from sleep.

and in the meantime: while something else was happening.

lifeboats: small boats carried on big ships to save passengers if the ship sinks.

band: a small orchestra.

2

Questions (to be answered after you have listened to the tape)

1 Describe the *Titanic*.
2 What sort of people was she carrying?
3 How many lives were lost?
4 Where was the *Titanic* when the disaster happened?
5 What was she doing that was dangerous?
6 Why was this dangerous?
7 Describe the weather that night.
8 What was the *Titanic* trying to do when it struck the iceberg?
9 Describe the damage that was done.
10 What happened on the other ship when the eight rockets were fired?

11 What was the captain of the *Californian* doing at the time?
12 What did the men on the *Californian* who saw the rockets think?
13 Why didn't more passengers get away in lifeboats?
14 What was happening up until the last few seconds on the *Titanic*? Why?

3

Summary

Use these short notes to summarise the main facts.

1 *Titanic*/most luxurious and biggest
2 some of the richest
3 maiden voyage
4 night of April 14th 1912/middle of the Atlantic
5 fast/dangerous
6 icebergs/slight mist
7 suddenly/iceberg/directly in front
8 trying to turn/struck/side torn open
9 another ship/nearby
10 eight white rockets
11 captain of the *Californian*/cabin/woken/told about the rockets
12 too sleepy/understand
13 five miles away/huge ship/sinking
14 dance band/dance music/passengers calm

4

Discussion (and/or extended writing)

Imagine you were on board the *Titanic* when it sank. Describe what happened.

Story/Dialogue

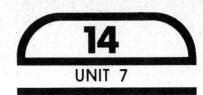

[Robert Wilson has a small disaster while he is on a skiing holiday in Switzerland.]

1

Story

Robert was skiing down a mountain with a tall, beautiful American girl. Her name was Isabel and he had met her only the day before. Isabel was a very good skier. The ski run twisted and turned but she went round all the curves very fast. Robert tried to do the same.

Suddenly, he fell. He felt a sharp pain in his ankle while he was lying in the snow. Isabel came back. Another skier, a handsome young man, stopped as well. The two of them helped Robert to get back to the hotel. There was a doctor there.

The doctor was a Scotsman. He was married to a Swiss girl. That was why he was working in Switzerland.

"Hmm," he said when he saw Robert's ankle, and shook his head.

"I haven't broken it, have I?" Robert asked hopefully.

"No, but you've twisted it badly."

"You mean, I've sprained it?"

"Yes, I'm afraid so. And it's badly bruised and swollen," the doctor answered, pointing to the dark blue marks on Robert's ankle, which was now getting bigger.

Robert lay back with a groan. No more skiing for him! Just then he heard Isabel laughing on the terrace. He could see her. She was smiling at the young man.

2

Multiple Choice

1 When you twist your ankle badly, you .... it.
   (a) break   (b) cut   •(c) pain   (d) sprain
2 The marks on Robert's ankle were .....
   (a) bruises   (b) cuts   (c) sprains   (d) breaks
3 The ankle was swollen. It was ....
   (a) bleeding   (b) broken   (c) getting bigger
   (d) very cold
4 When people groan, they are usually ....
   (a) angry   (b) excited   (c) interested   (d) unhappy

3

Questions

1 What was Robert doing when he fell?
2 Describe what happened then.
3 Who was Isabel?
4 How did Robert get back to the hotel?
5 Describe Robert's ankle.
6 Why was the doctor in Switzerland?
7 What exactly did the doctor tell Robert and what did Robert do?

       Practice

4a

What are the missing words?

They were skiing .... a ski run that .... and turned when Robert suddenly ..... He .... a .... pain .... his ankle. Back at the hotel, a Scots doctor .... was married .... a Swiss girl examined the ankle. He told Robert that he had .... it badly. In other words he had .... it. The ankle was badly b .... and s ....

4b

Combine these pairs.

| He was lying in the snow. He felt a pain in his ankle.
| He felt a pain in his ankle while he was lying in the snow.

1 He was skiing. He had an accident.
2 He was lying there. He saw her.
3 It was raining. He went out.
4 I was looking the other way. Someone kissed my wife.

4c

| Robert heard Isabel. She was laughing.
| Robert heard Isabel laughing.

1 He saw her. She was standing on the terrace.
2 He heard her. She was talking.
3 He smelt something. It was burning.
4 He felt something. It was running up his leg.
5 He watched a couple. They were dancing.

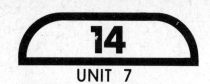

Dialogue/Practice

Listen to the complete dialogue. Then use this skeleton to reproduce what Robert says.

1

Dialogue

DOCTOR: Hmm.

ROBERT: .... painful.

DOCTOR: Try to move your foot up and down.

ROBERT: .... hurts ....

DOCTOR: Yes, but the important thing is that you can move it!

ROBERT: .... broken it, ...?

DOCTOR: No, but you've twisted it badly.

ROBERT: ....? .... sprained ....?

DOCTOR: Yes, I'm afraid so. And it's badly bruised and swollen.

ROBERT: .... other words .... skiing for me!

DOCTOR: No, I'm afraid not. You'll have to give it a good rest.

ROBERT: .... keep off ....?

DOCTOR: Yes. How does it feel now? Does it still hurt?

ROBERT: .... in fact, ... worse ....

DOCTOR: Well, I'll strap it up for you.

ROBERT: ....?

DOCTOR: Yes, I'll put something round it. A kind of bandage.

ROBERT: .... think .... something for the pain?

DOCTOR: Yes, if it really hurts that much. Er ... excuse me but that girl on the terrace ... just outside; who is she?

ROBERT: .... Isabel .... an American.

DOCTOR: Oh, she was coming out just as I came in, wasn't she?

ROBERT: Yes, ... right. She .... You see, we .... together when I .... the accident. She .... me .... to the hotel.

DOCTOR: Hmm. Very pretty, isn't she?

ROBERT: Yes, I suppose ....

2

Questions (about the rest of the conversation)
1 Where is Isabel during this conversation?
2 When did the doctor see her before?
3 What does the doctor say about her?

3

Vocabulary

Pick out from this dialogue:
1 the expressions that refer to various kinds of injuries
2 all the things you might ask a doctor to do if you are ever in the same situation
3 the questions here that you think almost any doctor would ask in a similar situation

 Practice

4a

Ask questions as Wilson did:

■ "I haven't broken it, have I?"

Ask the doctor if:
1 the sprain is very bad
2 it will take long to get better
3 you have to go to hospital
4 you have lost any blood
5 you have broken any bones
6 it is very serious

4b

Answer as the doctor does:

■ "I'm afraid so." "I'm afraid not."

1 Have I sprained my ankle?
2 Can I go skiing?
3 Will I have to stay in bed?
4 Can I go walking in the mountains?
5 Will it take long to get better?
6 Can I go dancing?
7 Can't you make it better?

5

Transfer

Now imagine you are Robert. Think of more questions yourself (at least eight) and then give the doctor's answers to them using either, "I'm afraid so" or "I'm afraid not".

Grammar Summary/Revision

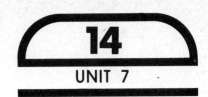

IRREGULAR VERBS

1a There are many types of irregular verb in English. It is important to learn and review this mechanical part of the language systematically and thoroughly. In this unit we shall give only a few of the types. More will be given in the following units. Those given here have occurred in this unit.

Type 1 Change in vowel only			**Type 2** Change in vowel in past and (e)n in participle		
strike	struck	have/had struck	break	broke	have/had broken
hold	held	held	know	knew	known
dig	dug	dug	tear	tore	torn
meet	met	met	see	saw	seen
			fall	fell	fallen
			lie	lay	lain

Type 3 Vowel change and final -t			**Type 4** Different vowels in past and in participle		
lose	lost	have/had lost	sink	sank	have/had sunk
feel	felt	felt	begin	began	begun
teach	taught	taught	sing	sang	sung

Exercise **1b** Now say whether these verbs belong to type 1, 2, 3, or 4. Give the past simple and participle forms of each.

find/win/sit/fight/get/shoot/write/rise/catch/bring/hear/ring/speak/forget/eat/keep

EXTENDED WRITING (and/or oral practice)

2a Work out a full conversation based on these facts.

You have hurt your wrist while horse riding. You are talking to a doctor. He asks you to move the wrist. You tell him it is painful to move it to the left or the right. You hope you have not broken it. The doctor says you have sprained it and that you must give it a good rest. In other words, you'll have to give up horse riding for a while. The pain is getting worse and you ask the doctor for something for it.

2b Disasters such as the *Titanic* are, unfortunately, not uncommon. Discuss, and then write about, a disaster which has happened recently. It might be a terrible plane or train crash, a flood, or a bridge which collapsed. Say what happened, why it happened, what was happening at the time, and perhaps also what people were doing, and what they did.

2c Almost everyone has had an accident at some time in the past – even if it wasn't a skiing accident like Robert's. Describe such an accident which you had once – however small or unimportant it was – and say what happened, what you were doing at the time, and so on.

LETTERS TO AN ADVICE COLUMN

The EBC recently did a programme about women's magazines. The readers of such magazines often write letters to them in which they ask for advice about problems.

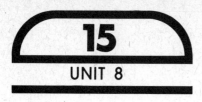

Alice Moore's ADVICE COLUMN

1

Dear Alice,

I am twenty and engaged. I love my fiancé very much. The problem is his father.

He is only forty. His wife is dead. He says he is in love with me and that he will kill himself unless I marry him. The situation is impossible. How can I marry my fiancé's father?

Unfortunately, I think I am in love with him as much as I am with his son.

I want to tell my fiancé all about this, but if I do, he will be hurt and angry. Whatever I do, it seems I'll hurt either him or his father. What would you do if you were me?

Yours sincerely,

Veronica M (Basingstoke)

2

ALICE'S REPLY

You sound like a confused and silly girl to me. How can you possibly be in love with two men at the same time? If you really loved your fiancé, you would not be in love with his father!

If I were you, I'd tell my fiancé about all this immediately. Of course he will be hurt! But he'll be even more hurt if he finds out about you from someone else! Unless you tell him yourself, he'll lose faith in you completely.

Questions

Imagine you are interviewing first Veronica from Basingstoke and then Alice Moore. Find questions and then answers.

a Find out:

1 how old Veronica is
2 how she feels about her fiancé
3 how old his father is
4 what his father says he will do
5 how she feels about the father
6 if she has told her fiancé yet
7 why not
8 why she doesn't do something immediately

b Find out:

1 what Alice thinks of Veronica
2 why she thinks Veronica doesn't really love both men
3 what she would do if she were Veronica
4 why she would do this
5 what she thinks will happen if Veronica does not do this

3

Dear Alice,

I love my boyfriend, but there's a problem. He seems to love his mother more than me.

Whenever we go out, he takes her along. Wherever we go, she goes, too. Whatever we do, she does as well. I wouldn't put up with this for a moment if I didn't love him so much.

We're going to get married soon. I'm afraid that when we do, his mother will come to live with us. What can I do?

Yours sincerely,

Betty S (Manchester)

4

ALICE'S REPLY

You and your boyfriend can't sacrifice your lives to his mother. Unless he realises this, you'll both be very unhappy. I am sure that if he really loves you, he'll understand this. If I were you, I'd tell him exactly that.

Questions

a

Interview Betty S. Ask her:

1 why she thinks her boyfriend loves his mother more than her
2 what happens when they go out
3 what else his mother does that causes trouble
4 why she puts up with it
5 if they plan to get married soon
6 what she thinks will happen then

b

Ask Alice:

1 what Betty's boyfriend must realise
2 why
3 if she thinks he'll understand this
4 what she would do if she were Betty

Practice

Women sometimes write to advice columns about problems like this.

What is the man doing here? Why?

Now say what you *would* do if you *were* the man.
What would you do if you were the woman?

Say what you think will happen if:

1 he spills oil on the carpet
2 he brings his motor bike in as well
3 she orders him to take the mower into the shed immediately

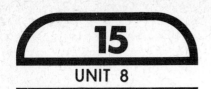

If I tell my fiancé, he'll be hurt and angry.

If you really loved your fiancé you wouldn't be in love with his father.

1a

Imagine Veronica is talking to you.

> VERONICA: **Perhaps I'll write to Alice Moore. Will she give me good advice?**
> YOU: **Yes, if you *write* to Alice, I'm sure she*'ll give you* good advice.**

Notice that you use the simple present (*write*) in the if-clause.

1 Perhaps I'll write to Alice. Do you think she'll answer?
2 Perhaps I'll tell my boyfriend. But will he understand?
3 I'll go to him now. But will he listen?
4 I'll be very honest. Will he forgive me?
5 I'll marry him. Do you think we'll have a happy life?
6 Or perhaps I'll marry his father. I wonder if I'll be unhappy.

This is called the future conditional. If one thing happens now or later, something else will happen as a result.

1b

Transfer

You have to get to New York immediately. If you do, you'll get a very good job. But the company won't wait. Say what will happen if you do these things.

1 You can go either by ship or by plane.
2 Or you could try to swim across. It's much cheaper. (You swim badly.)
3 You haven't got a passport. Why not go without one?
4 Or why not simply tell the people there to wait a few months?

Now think of more examples. For example, what will happen if you: don't study, fall asleep during the lesson, kiss the boss's secretary or the boss himself, etc.

2a

This is the unreal present. We use the if-clause and the past tense for things that are impossible (because they are contrary to present fact). The other clause shows why they are impossible. Imagine you and your friend are talking about such impossibilities.

> YOUR FRIEND: **Can this be a real diamond? It costs £1.**
> YOU: **I don't think so. If it *were* a real diamond, it *would cost* more than that.**

1 Does my boyfriend really love me? He goes out with other girls.
2 Does Veronica really want to marry me? She says she loves my father.
3 Are those people really English? They speak with French accents.
4 Do you think that man really has a lot of money? His clothes are very shabby.
5 Does that French student really want to learn English? He talks French all the time.
6 Is this meat really fresh? It has a strange smell.

Note that the verb form in the if-clause is the same as the past simple. Only *be* is slightly different. *Were* can be used for all persons.

2b

Transfer

You don't live in London but you want to. Think of all the things you*'d have to do* and which you*'d be able to do* if you *did*.

> Example: **"If I lived in London, I'd have to travel in crowded buses, but I'd be able to see lots of plays."**

Think of more examples!

Unless you tell him yourself, he'll lose faith in you completely.

Whenever we go out, wherever we go, whatever we do ...

3a

Imagine you are talking to a doctor. Note the *affirmative verb* after *unless*.

> DOCTOR: **Get some rest. Or do you want to have a nervous breakdown?**
>
> YOU: **You mean, *unless* I *get* some rest, I'll have a nervous breakdown?**

1   Find another job. Or do you want to have a heart attack?
2   Take these tablets. Or do you want to fall ill?
3   Stop eating meat. Or do you want to die?
4   See me tomorrow. If you don't, you'll get worse.

3b

Transfer

You have a secretary. You'll have to sack her, or lower her salary, or give her another job unless she does certain things. You are talking to her. Make sentences like, "Unless you . . . , I'll have to . . ." You want her to:

1   improve her typing
2   take shorter coffee breaks
3   learn shorthand
4   call you "Sir"
5   speak more politely
6   learn how to spell
7   stop phoning her boyfriend
8   come on time

Think of more examples yourself.

4a

You are talking to Betty S, who wrote the second letter.

> BETTY: **Whenever I say something, my boyfriend's mother always disagrees.**

Now make more sentences with *whenever/whatever/wherever*.

1   Where we go, she goes.
2   She does everything we do.
3   When I see him, she's always with him.
4   When I kiss him, he always tells her.
5   When we go dancing, she always dances with him.

4b

Transfer

For some strange reason, a detective has been following you. For example, when you look around, he's always there.

> You say: **Whenever I turn around, he's always there.**

What else happens? For instance:

1   You say something, and he notes it down.
2   You go somewhere; he always follows you.
3   You make phone calls; he listens.
4   You get letters; they're open.

Make more sentences about yourself and this detective.

Alice Moore is really a journalist. She explains how she came to do this sort of work.

1

Vocabulary

career: way of making a living, profession.

fashion: the latest styles in clothes.

troubles: (here) problems, the things that bother you.

take over: (here) do the job another person did before.

out of touch with: (here) had no contact with, did not really understand.

nervous breakdown: a kind of nervous crisis.

too involved, wrapped up in: (here) to think too much about something. Example: "He's so wrapped up in his work that he has no time for anything else "

genuine: real, what it is said to be.

Mack Sennet: film director famous for early Hollywood comedy films (Keystone Cops).

pie: fruit or sometimes meat covered with pastry and then baked.

2

Questions (to be answered after you have heard the tape)

1 How did Alice begin her career? What sort of articles did she write?
2 When did she take over the advice column and what was it called then?
3 Why was it called this?
4 Why did Alice take over the column from the older woman?
5 What sort of people write letters to the column?
6 Why did 'Aunt Margaret' have a nervous breakdown?
7 What is the question the interviewer asks about the readers' letters?
8 What else does he say about them?
9 Does Alice personally think they are amusing?
10 She describes a scene from a typical comedy film. Describe the scene yourself.

11 What is the question she asks after this? What is the answer?
12 What is the very last thing she says about the readers' letters?

3

Summary

Use these short notes to summarise the main points.

1 Alice Moore/ the column ten years ago
2 called "Dear Aunt Margaret" then because
3 Aunt Margaret/much older
4 many people felt/too old
5 out of touch/younger people
6 something else as well/nervous breakdown because/wrapped up
7 all the letters/genuine
8 not amusing/people who write them
9 like a scene/comedy film
10 someone/pie/another person's face/But if someone/*your* face/not laugh

4

Discussion (and/or extended writing)

Describe some scenes from comedies that are funny only to the people who see the things happening but not to the people to whom they actually happen.

Story/Dialogue

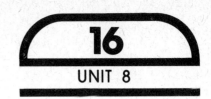
Linda went into a department store to buy a raincoat. This is what happened.

1

Story

As soon as Linda went into the department that sold raincoats, she sensed there was something unusual in the atmosphere.

First of all, there was a salesman there and not a saleswoman. That was very unusual in the women's coat department. He asked if he could be of any help. But when she said she was just looking he did not seem to be listening. He did not look very much like a salesman, either.

A second later a raincoat caught her eye. She asked him a question about it. He did not even hear her at first. She asked again. She wanted to know if he had any coats like it with a detachable lining. He did not seem to understand what a detachable lining was. She explained. Then she went on looking. She noticed that the salesman seemed to be watching another customer in the department all the time. The other customer, a middle-aged woman, left the department. The salesman immediately went to the phone and told somebody on the other end that the woman had gone and had definitely taken two leather belts without paying for them. Then he turned to Linda and explained that he was not a salesman at all but a store detective. Later, Linda read in the paper that a woman had been arrested for stealing some belts from a department store, or, in other words, for shoplifting.

2

Multiple Choice

1   *Sense* here means . . . .
    (a) feel   (b) smell   (c) hear   (d) listen
2   *Lining* here is . . . .
    (a) stuff   (b) special material   (c) lines
    (d) the material inside the coat
3   *Detachable* here means that you can . . . .
    (a) take it out   (b) tie it   (c) close it   (d) wash it
4   The other customer stole things from shops.
    She was a shop . . . .
    (a) thief   (b) robber   (c) lifter   (d) elevator

3

Questions

1   What was the first unusual thing Linda noticed?
2   What was the first thing Linda said?
3   What was the salesman's reaction?
4   What did she ask him a few seconds later?
5   What was strange about the salesman's reaction then?
6   What did Linda notice then?
7   What happened after that?

   Practice

4a

You go into a shop but you don't want a salesman to follow you around; you want to look. What do you say?

4b

Transform the "kernels" into result sentences.

She left. She did not pay.
She left without paying.

1   She came in. She did not knock.
2   He walked five miles. He did not stop.
3   He spoke for ten minutes. He did not pause.
4   I lay there for five hours. I did not go to sleep.

4c

The woman had stolen some belts and was arrested. In other words:

She was arrested for stealing some belts.

What were these people arrested for?

1   A bank clerk stole £5,000.
2   A woman threw some paint at the Prime Minister.
3   Another woman shot her husband.
4   An old man took off all his clothes in a public park.
5   Two Irishmen got into a fight and smashed up a pub.

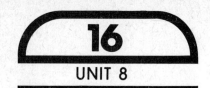

16

UNIT 8

Listen to the dialogue. Then reproduce what Linda says.

1

Dialogue

LINDA: Excuse .... Have .... coats .... this .... detachable ....?

SALESMAN: I beg your pardon?

LINDA: Have .... like this with ....?

SALESMAN: A what?

LINDA: A .... lining. You know, the sort .... you can .... out .... the coat.

SALESMAN: I, uh, I'm not sure really. I mean, I don't really know.

LINDA: .... you? Well, then, is .... someone here who ....?

SALESMAN: Well, the salesgirl in this department has gone to lunch. I don't usually work here.

LINDA: .... lunch? When .... back?

SALESMAN: In, uh, a few minutes.

LINDA: I see. This coat .... a price .... I don't .... you know how much ....?

SALESMAN: Uh, £20, I think.

LINDA: £20? For a .... this? .... cheaper?

SALESMAN: There are some more coats over there.

LINDA: I see. (*She looks through them*) Now this .... exactly .... looking for! .... I .... on?

SALESMAN: Excuse me for one moment, madam. (*He picks up the phone*) Hello? This is Watson. I'm in the women's coat department. That woman has just left with two belts, and she hasn't paid for them. Arrest her! (*to Linda*) I'm sorry, madam. I'm not a salesman.

LINDA: .... not?

SALESMAN: No, I'm a store detective. I've been following a shoplifter all over the store.

Practice

2a

What does Linda say to show that she wants:
1 the salesman's attention
2 to see if the coat fits
3 something cheaper

2b

Respond as Linda does.

SALESMAN: **I don't know.**
LINDA: *Don't* **you? Well, is there someone here who** *does?*

1 I can't help you.
2 I'm not serving customers.
3 I haven't got any time.
4 I won't serve you!
5 I don't know anything about coats.
6 I'm not able to help you.

2c

Linda asks:

"I don't suppose you know how much it is?"

You are Linda. Use the same pattern to ask:
1 what size the coat is
2 what it's made of
3 where the salesgirl is
4 where the public telephone is
5 when the store closes
6 who that strange man is

3

Transfer

You are talking to a ticket collector at a railway station. He is very unhelpful. Ask him questions beginning, "I don't suppose you know . . .?" Ask him:
1 when the next train to London is
2 when it arrives
3 if there's a dining car
4 if it's usually very full
5 if it's on time

Think of other questions you might ask him.

Grammar Summary/Revision

16

UNIT 8

IRREGULAR VERBS
(Revision)

1a In unit 7 we reviewed four types of irregular verb. Give a few examples from each type!

1b Further classification of irregular verbs.

Type 5			**Type 6**		
No change at all			Vowel change, and final -d		
hurt	hurt	have/had hurt	tell	told	have/had told
cost	cost	cost	hear	heard	heard
let	let	let			

Type 7			**Type 8**
Vowel change in past only			Final -d changes to -t, or -t is added.
run	ran	have/had run	send sent have/had sent

Type 9
Participle in -t or -d
learn	learned	have/had learned
	learnt	have/had learnt

Exercise **1c** Give the past and participle forms for each of these verbs. Use them in examples.

come/put/build/say/cut/shut/become/sell/lend/hit/speed

REPORTED SPEECH
(final notes)

2a Did you notice this in Letter 1?

> **My fiancé's father has told me that he *cannot* go on living without me. I have told him that our love *is* impossible.**

When *say*, *tell*, *explain*, etc. are in the present simple or present perfect, there is no change in the tense in reported speech.

Exercise **2b** Study this dialogue.

> A: **I love you.**
> B: **What did you say?**
> A: **I said I loved you!**
> B: **(a few seconds later) Tell me . . . do you really love me?**
> A: **Of course I do! I've just told you that I love you!**

Paired Practice **2c** With someone else, use the dialogue above as a "frame" for more conversations just like that. A should begin with these statements.

1 I want to kill myself.
2 I hate you.
3 I've just seen a ghost.
4 It's raining.
5 The Queen is standing outside.
6 I've won a million dollars.

EXTENDED WRITING
(and/or oral practice)

3a Write short letters to an advice column for:

1 a man who loves football and whose wife hates it so much that she will not let him watch it!
2 a seventeen year old girl whose old-fashioned father will not allow her to go out with boys!
3 a woman whose husband thinks only of his work.
4 a man whose mother tries to make all his decisions for him.

3b Discuss these statements

1 It's a woman's job and duty to follow her husband everywhere and do whatever he wants without complaining.
2 We must take care of our parents when they get old even if it means sacrificing our own happiness.

17
UNIT 9

LIFE IN THE FUTURE

1

What will life be like in 100 years' time? By then, the population of the world will have doubled. We will have run out of many essential materials like oil and coal. We may even have run out of water to drink. Some experts believe that we will be living like these chickens. We will be living in little boxes and eating artificial food.

Questions

Imagine you are interviewing an expert about the future. Find out:

1 how much larger the population of the world will be
2 if we will have run out of some materials
3 if there are other things we *may* have run out of
4 how we *may* be living
5 what we *may* be eating

Answer the questions as well.

2

Some experts are pessimistic. Others are far more optimistic. They say that life will be far better than it is today. We may be living in cities like this. We may be getting far more sunlight, breathing fresher air, living in better buildings and leading far better lives than we are today.

Questions

a

Now imagine you are interviewing a more optimistic expert. Notice the questions and answers.

Ask a question with the words "better than it is today".

YOU: Do you think life will be better than it is today?

THE EXPERT: Yes, I think it will *or* Yes, I think it may.

b

Now ask questions ending with the words:

1 in cities like this?
2 getting more sunlight?
3 breathing fresher air?
4 in better buildings?
5 leading better lives?

3

Life will certainly have become far more mechanised. It may even have become too mechanised. Mechanisation has already caused quite a few problems and will cause still more. For example, many jobs will have been "automated". That is, machines will be doing many jobs that people do today. People will no longer be able to learn only one job in their lifetimes. They will have to learn several. Many of the jobs that young people are doing today will have become unnecessary by the time they are forty. This problem will have grown in 100 years' time.

Questions

Ask the expert questions beginning, "Do you think . . . ?" using these words.

1 Life—more mechanised in the future?
2 Too mechanised?
3 Mechanisation—already caused problems?
4 Cause still more?
5 Will machines—jobs that people do today?
6 Only one job in their lifetimes?
7 Some jobs—become unnecessary?
8 This problem—grown in 100 years' time?

4

Discussion

a

In 100 years' time, all sorts of things will or may have happened. What are some of them? For example, think of such things as:

1 a cure for cancer
2 space travel; the other planets
3 atomic power

Robots may have become very common in 100 years. This cartoon shows what may be happening then.

What is happening here?
Does the man look happy?
Why not?

b

What are some of the things you think robots may be doing for us in 100 years' time?

What is happening now?

How does the man look now?
Why?

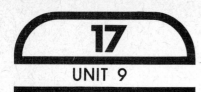

We'll be living in little boxes in 100 years' time.

1a

The future continuous can be used to focus on a fragment of a complete act. People will be living in little boxes not only in 100 years' time. It will probably be going on before that and after that point in time.

Now imagine you are talking to a friend. He is going to begin something in a few seconds. You are going to leave and come back in two hours' time.

> YOUR FRIEND: **I'm going to type these letters now.**
> YOU: **Will you be typing them when I get back?**

Ask more questions like this. Your friend says:

1 I'm going to watch television.
2 I'm going to do this work.
3 I think I'll wash these clothes now.
4 I'll just sit here.
5 I'll wait here.
6 I'll write some letters.

1b

Transfer

Your friend wants to phone you tomorrow. He is trying to find a good time to call.

> YOUR FRIEND: **I'll phone at 6 tomorrow evening. Will that be all right?**
> YOU: **At 6? No, I'll be eating dinner then.**

Think of other things you will or may be doing at certain times tomorrow. For example, he wants to phone you at:

1 5 in the morning
2 8 o'clock
3 10 o'clock
4 12 noon
5 3 in the afternoon
6 9 in the evening

We may be getting far more sunlight and living in better cities.

2

May be doing is used here for what possibly may be going on at some time in the future. You probably do not know for certain but describe where you may be working, what you may be doing, where you may be living:

1 two years from now
2 when you're sixty-five
3 this time next year
4 this time tomorrow
5 next weekend at 5 in the afternoon

The population of the world will have doubled in 100 years' time.

3

The future perfect is used for things that will be complete, will already have happened by the time a certain point in the future is reached.

Now imagine your teacher is talking to you. He is telling you that certain things must be done before a point in the future.

> YOUR TEACHER: **You're going to have a test next week. Learn all these words.**
> YOU: **All right. I'll have learned them by then.**

Give more answers like this. Your teacher says:

1 Do this test now. It must be finished in an hour's time.
2 Finish this homework. I'll collect it in half an hour.
3 Answer all these questions before 5.
4 Read this book. But I want it back at the end of the week.
5 Write a composition about the future. Do it before next Monday.
6 You must get through the book before the term ends.

 We may have run out of water to drink.

4a

May again introduces the idea that something is possible; that we cannot be certain. Here, Wilson is speaking to his secretary, Margaret Dickinson.

WILSON: **Can you type all these letters? I must have them before 6.**
MARGARET: **Well, I *may have typed* them all by then. I can't be sure.**

Reply as Margaret did. Wilson says:

1 Finish all this work by this evening!
2 Do you think you can do it before 5?
3 Type this interview before noon.
4 Oh, and you must make all these phone calls before I get back.
5 And book my tickets before lunch.

4b

Transfer

You cannot look into the future but you can probably imagine many of the things you will have done or may have done in ten years' time. What are they? For example, people get married, have children, get better jobs, move to different countries, learn languages, etc.

4c

Comment

May have done can be used in the past, too. It can mean, "Perhaps this happened or has happened". Notice how Margaret uses it here.

ROBERT: **My airline ticket still hasn't arrived. It was sent five days ago.**
MARGARET: **Well, it *may have got* lost in the post.**

What does she say if she thinks that perhaps:

1 the postman delivered it to the office downstairs
2 the airline sent it to the wrong person
3 the airline has forgotten to post it
4 it has come in this morning's post
5 she has put it on his desk
6 someone has taken it away by mistake

4d

Transfer

You have arranged to meet a friend in front of a coffee shop at 4 o'clock. It is 4.15. You are there but your friend is not. Why? Think of possible explanations with *may have . . . .* For example: perhaps he forgot about it, or has had an accident, or his car has broken down, etc.

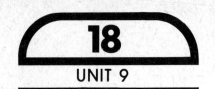 **Intensive Listening**

 18

UNIT 9

An economist is interviewed about automation.

1

Vocabulary

predictions: opinions, statements about what will happen in the future.

consumers: the buying public.

computer programmer: a specialist in giving information to a computer.

dull, monotonous, routine work: boring work with nothing new about it.

assembly line: line along which a product is put together in stages.

handle (verb): (here) take care of, do.

to a certain extent: partly.

trade (noun): (here) the type of job a worker does. Example: "I'm a mechanic; that's my trade."

professions: jobs requiring a high degree of training, like medicine, law, architecture, etc.

2

Questions (to be answered after you have listened to the tape)

1 What is the interviewer's very first question?
2 Does the economist say all factory work will be automated?
3 What other type of work will have been automated?
4 What do you think he means by the phrase "at a more simple level"?
5 Is it only simple clerical work that will have been automated in offices?
6 Does the economist actually say that computers will be taking decisions for us?
7 What kinds of predictions can a computer make?
8 What use are these predictions to a manager?
9 What does the interviewer want to know about "ordinary people"?
10 What answer is given? Will computers simply destroy jobs?
11 What does the economist say about "dull, monotonous, routine work"?

12 What example of it does he give?
13 What can be done with people whose jobs have been automated?
14 What is the economist's prediction?

3

Summary

Use these short notes to summarise the main points.

1 100 years' time/a lot of factory work/clerical work
2 computers/predictions/consumers will be buying
3 this information/managers/decisions
4 a lot of new jobs/created/but/dull, monotonous routine work/machines
5 for example/machines/handle/assembly line
6 possible/predict/100 years' time/man is sixty/possibly three trades or professions

4

Discussion

1 Give other examples of work which you think can easily be automated or should be automated.
2 What would happen if we automated all the jobs we possibly could in the shortest possible time? What would be the social results?
3 How do you personally feel about the idea of being trained for three different trades or professions before you are sixty?

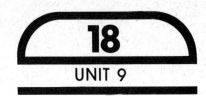

Robert Wilson has an argument with a very important person in the EBC.

1

Story

The man sitting opposite Robert was the Financial Controller. Everybody called him "the FC" for short. He made all the decisions about money. Robert needed some more. That was why he had to see him. The two men did not get on very well. In fact, they had always disliked each other.

"Your request is out of the question," the FC said. Robert had difficulty in controlling himself, but he managed somehow. He explained that he wanted the money in order to make more programmes.

"And why do you want to do that?" the FC asked sharply. Again, Robert almost lost his temper. "Because more and more people are listening to my department's programmes. There's a great demand for them," he answered.

The FC did not seem to believe him. But Robert had a report on the numbers of listeners to all EBC programmes. The FC became less confident. Robert threw the report down on the table and told him to read it.

The FC looked at it in silence. The figures proved that he had been wrong, but he did not want to admit it. "Well," he finally said, "I may have made a small mistake." Robert noticed the word 'may'. He got up to leave. But he had the feeling that he would get the money after all.

2

Vocabulary

What are the missing words?

1 Robert did not like the FC. He did not . . . . with him.
2 Robert got angry. He could hardly . . . . himself.
3 A lot of people listened to Robert's programmes. There was a great . . . . them.
4 At first, the FC was very *sure of himself.* In other words, he was very . . . .
5 He could see from the figures that he was wrong. They . . . . he was wrong.
6 But he didn't want to . . . . it.

3

Questions

1 Who was the FC?
2 Why did Robert want to see him?
3 How did they feel about each other?
4 What didn't the FC seem to believe?
5 Why did he become less confident?
6 What happened at the end?

Practice

4a

Use these verbs with either *each other* or *themselves.* Like this:

▌ disliked – **They disliked each other.**

1 both men hated
2 they tried to control
3 they didn't trust
4 they shouted at
5 argued with
6 looked at
7 defended
8 attacked
9 almost hit
10 finally left

4b

Transfer

A young man and woman want to get married. Why? Give reasons with:

1 love
2 adore
3 worship
4 can't live without
5 trust
6 never argue with

Can you think of more such examples?

4c

Now combine these pairs like this.

▌ **The man was the FC. He was sitting opposite Robert.**
The man sitting opposite Robert was the FC.

1 That woman is my wife. She's sitting over there.
2 That thing is my book. It's lying on the floor.
3 The girl was a princess. She was sitting on my lap.
4 That man is a millionaire. He is wearing a shabby raincoat.

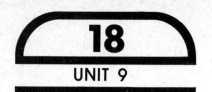

Dialogue/Practice

18

UNIT 9

Listen to the complete dialogue. Then reproduce Robert's part.

Practice

1

Dialogue

FC: And now, about your request. I'm afraid it's out of the question.

ROBERT: .... question? But I .... that money .... more programmes.

FC: And why do you want to do that?

ROBERT: Why .... more programmes?

FC: Yes, you must have a reason.

ROBERT: But I ....! More and more people .... my department's programmes. There's a .... for them!

FC: Oh, come now. You can't be sure of that.

ROBERT: But ....! .... you .... the audience figures lately?

FC: Yes, of course I have. I've already studied them.

ROBERT: Really? You don't seem to .... studied them ....!

FC: What do you mean? I'm sure your audience figures didn't go up at all last month.

ROBERT: But ....! .... you .... the .... report?

FC: The latest report? Of course not. It hasn't come out yet.

ROBERT: But it ....! It .... yesterday evening. I happen .... with me! Here! .... at it!

The Financial Controller looks at the report

ROBERT: The report .... that the figures .... up all the time! They .... doubled .... end .... year.

FC: Well, I may have made a small mistake.

ROBERT: A .... one? It doesn't .... so .... me! You .... wrong .... figures. Why can't you ....?

FC: I, er, I'll have to give the matter some more thought.

ROBERT: And .... meantime I'll .... programmes!

2a

Robert asks the FC:

"**Do you happen to have seen the audience figures lately?**"

In the same way ask if he has:
1 watched any programmes
2 heard any good jokes
3 seen Linda
4 talked to her

2b

Transfer

You are a doctor. Something mental or physical, you don't know which, is wrong with a patient. Ask him questions beginning, "Do you happen to have .... lately?" Ask about:
1 strange food
2 in any foreign countries
3 strange medicines
4 trouble at work or at home

Think of more such questions.

2c

FC: **I've already studied them.**

ROBERT: **Really? You don't seem to have studied them at all!**

1 I've read that report.
2 I've examined the figures.
3 I've looked into the matter.
4 I've heard about it.
5 I've looked at the figures.

3

Transfer

You are a teacher. You are making comments about what your students *seem to have done* or *don't seem to have done* in the last few months. For example, you think one student has made a lot of progress, another has worked hard, another has not understood anything. What do you say?

Grammar Summary/Revision

INFINITIVE FORMS

1a Observe how we can combine verbs like *seem*, *appear*, and *happen* with three forms of the infinitive.

1 He understands the figures (seem)   He seems to understand the figures.
2 He is studying them now (appear)   He appears to be studying them now.
3 He has finished (seem)   He seems to have finished.
4 He finished (seem)   He seems to have finished.

Comment 1b The three forms of the infinitive are:

1 the simple infinitive (*to understand*).
2 the progressive or continuous infinitive (*to be studying*).
3 the perfective infinitive (*to have finished*).

1c Now combine these forms yourself.

1 They are arguing (seem)
2 They dislike each other (seem)
3 He has lost his temper (appear)
4 He has the figures with him (happen)
5 He got the report yesterday (happen)
6 The FC has not seen them (seem)
7 Robert is winning the argument (appear)
8 The FC has made a mistake (seem)

EXTENDED WRITING
(and/or oral practice)

2 Work out a dialogue based on these facts.

You are a salesman who travels about for a large firm. They give all their salesmen a car for this purpose. You want a larger one. You have to get it from the sales director. He tells you it is out of the question. But you need it in order to impress customers. You tell him that your sales figures are going up all the time. He does not seem to believe you. You happen to have a copy of the latest sales report and you ask him if he has seen it. He does not even know it has come out yet. The figures show that your sales doubled last month and may have tripled (gone up by 300%) by the end of the year. The sales director does not want to admit he has made a mistake. You get angry and tell him you will find another job if he does not give you the bigger car. Then you walk out.

DISCUSSION
(and/or extended writing)

3 Are you optimistic or pessimistic about the future? Say why. In particular, talk about *any one* or *all three* of these questions.

1 What will happen if more and more people lose their jobs because of automation?
2 Suppose the population of the world doubles or triples; what will life be like in such a crowded world?
3 What will happen if, soon, everybody has a motor car and there is very little public transport (buses, underground trains, etc.)?

Crime and Punishment

1

If you had been alive 200 years ago, and perhaps had stolen only a few loaves of bread, you would have gone to prison. If you had killed someone, something far worse would have happened to you. You would have been hanged in public. Life was hard and often brutal. So was the law. Perhaps it had to be. If you had lived in a large city like London, and if you had walked through the streets at night, someone might have killed you only in order to get your money.

Questions

a

Ask questions; give answers. You are interviewing an expert on crime.
You know that:

1 people were hanged in public 200 years ago; ask why

2 something happened to people who stole bread; ask what

3 the law was hard; ask why

4 things happened to people who walked through the streets at night; ask what

b

Now tell someone else what would have happened to them 200 years ago if:

1 they had stolen some bread

2 killed someone

3 walked through the streets at night

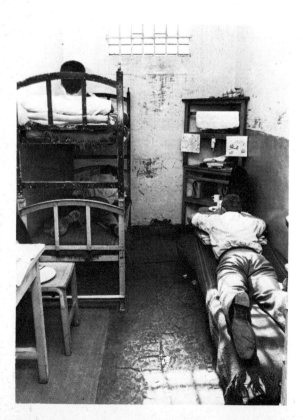

2

Prisons have of course got much better in the last 200 years. But conditions are still far from perfect. If you were in a prison in many countries today, you would probably be living in a cell like this. You would probably be sharing it with at least two other people. Many people say, "Why should criminals have any better conditions? They shouldn't have broken the law in the first place!"

Questions

You are still interviewing the expert.
Find out:

1 if prisons have got any better in the last 200 years

2 if conditions are perfect

3 what sort of cell you would be living in if you were in prison

4 how many people you would be sharing it with

5 what people say about such conditions

3

The driver of this car had been to a party before the accident happened. He had had a lot to drink. He was driving home when the accident happened. He suddenly lost control of the car and ran into a bus stop and then a wall. Luckily, nobody was standing there because a bus had come by only a minute before. It had picked up ten people. In other words, if the accident had happened only a minute before, the man would have killed someone. He should not have drunk so much. He might have killed ten people.

Of course, he did not know the accident was going to happen or that he would hit the bus stop. But what should the law have done if he had killed someone? Would the man have been a murderer?

Questions

a

Ask and answer.
You are interviewing a policeman who saw the accident.
You know that:

1 the man had been somewhere; ask where

2 he had had something to drink; ask how much

3 he was going somewhere; ask where

4 he ran into the bus stop; ask why

5 nobody was killed; ask why

6 something might have happened if the bus hadn't come by; ask what

Give the answers as well.

b

Now ask the policeman:

1 if ten people definitely would have been killed

2 if the man knew what was going to happen

Imagine the policeman's answers.

c

What are the last two questions about the law?
How would you answer them?

d

Now say what would have happened or what might not have happened if:

1 the man had not drunk so much

2 he had not lost control of the car

3 a bus had not come by a minute before

4 ten people had been standing at the stop

Grammar Exposition and Exercises

The past conditional (for unreal conditions)

Continuous conditional forms

1a

Note the transformation.

He was drunk; that's why he lost control of the car.
If he *hadn't been* drunk, he *wouldn't have lost* control of the car.

Comment

1 In the if-clause, a *past* form is transformed into the *past perfect*.
2 In the main clause, a *past* form is transformed into *would have (done)*.

1b

Transform these pairs in the same way.

1 I got up late. I missed the bus.
2 I missed the bus. I was late for work.
3 I was late for work. That's why the boss was angry.
4 The boss got angry. That's why he shouted at me.
5 He shouted at me so I shouted at him.
6 I shouted at him and I lost my job.

1c

Transfer

A month ago, you went out without an umbrella, got wet, caught a cold, fell ill and lost your job. A week later you found a much better job. How many sentences can you make from this story beginning, "If I hadn't ...., I ...."? Can you think of a similar story yourself?

2a

| He | was driving | so fast that he | lost | control of the car. |

| If he | hadn't been driving | so fast, he | wouldn't have lost | control of the car. |

| He | was | in a hurry; that's why he | was driving | so fast. |

| If he | hadn't been | in a hurry, he | wouldn't have been driving | so fast. |

2b

Now transform these pairs.

1 I was standing there. That's why I saw the accident.
2 He was driving fast. That's why he had an accident.
3 He was drunk. That's why he was driving dangerously.
4 A policeman was driving past. He saw the accident.
5 He left work early. That's why he was driving past.
6 The man didn't know about the policeman. That's why he was driving fast.

2c

Transfer

You saw the accident because you were standing at the corner. You were waiting for a bus. Your mother had asked you to visit her. You wanted to give her some flowers. It was her birthday. That's why you were waiting for the bus. How many sentences beginning, "If .... hadn't ...., ... wouldn't have ...." can you make from this situation?

**He shouldn't have drunk so much at the party.
He might have killed ten people.**

3a

Comment

Might have done shows that something *could have happened* in the past but *did not*.
Should have done is simply the past of *should* or *ought* as in, "You should (ought to) do this work now; in fact, you should (ought to) have done it a long time ago!"

3b

Now answer as B does here.

**A: I drove very fast but I didn't have an accident.
B: Yes, but you might have had an accident! That's why you shouldn't have driven so fast!**

1 I ran out into the street without looking and nothing happened to me.
2 I drank five bottles of whisky and I did not die afterwards.
3 I shouted at the boss but he did not sack me.
4 I didn't set the alarm clock and I didn't oversleep the next morning, either.
5 They built the house with very cheap materials and it didn't fall down.
6 I didn't lock my car last night but it wasn't stolen.

He didn't know the accident *was going to happen* or that he *would hit* the bus stop.

4

Comment

1 Both *was/were going to do* and *would do* are used as *future in the past* forms. There is rarely, if ever, any real difference in meaning between them. (Compare the ordinary future forms with *going to* and *will*.)

2 *Future in the past* here means that, at the point in the past that we are referring to, the event is in the future; but looking back from the present, it is in the past. (If the man got into his car at 3 o'clock yesterday, and the accident happened at 3.30, then at 3 o'clock the accident was still in the future – but now, today, it is in the past.)

 Practice

5a

Read this short story.

The sun was shining when I got up that morning, so I decided to go for a walk in the country. I walked for about two miles. Then, suddenly, black clouds covered the sun. It began to rain. I stood under a tree. Suddenly lightning struck the tree. I was not hurt but I began to run. I ran across a small bridge over a stream. The bridge collapsed. I fell into the stream. I got terribly wet. I took a bus home. The bus broke down. I caught a terrible cold. I decided that I would never take a walk in the country again.

5b

1 Make as many sentences as you can from this story beginning, "I had no idea (or "I didn't know") that . . . . was going to (or would) . . . ."
2 Now make sentences beginning, "If I'd known that . . . . was going to . . . ., I would never have . . . ."
3 Can you tell or write such a story in which a series of unfortunate things happened to you? Can you also then use it to make a number of sentences beginning, "I didn't know . . . ." and "If I'd known . . . .?"

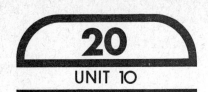

Intensive Listening

20

UNIT 10

A magistrate is interviewed.

A magistrate is a kind of judge who deals with people who have committed small crimes. The magistrate describes a man who got into trouble shortly after he came out of prison.

1

Vocabulary

come before: a criminal who *comes before* a judge is *dealt with* by that judge.

He had only just come out of prison: he had come out of prison only a short time ago.

break into: get into a house illegally.

feed (verb): give food to or get food for someone.

case: (here) all the facts and circumstances surrounding the man's crime.

look down on: the way one person behaves when he thinks another person is inferior or bad. "Snobs look down on poor people."

feel tempted to do something: feel a very strong desire or urge to do something.

sentence (noun): the judge sentences a criminal who has been found guilty; he gives him some sort of punishment. "He was given a sentence of three years in prison."

definitely: without doubt.

2

Questions

1 What had happened before the man came before the judge?
2 What sort of place did the man live in and what was his problem?
3 What sort of crime had he committed?
4 Do you think the man did this simply because he didn't want to work? Why?
5 Why did the man say he had committed the crime?
6 Why does the judge think the man committed the crime?
7 In what way would prison be better for the man in the man's own opinion?
8 What was it that the judge could not help doing when he heard the man's case?
9 What does the judge say he would have done if he had been in the man's place?
10 What would have made the judge do this?
11 What did the judge finally do with the man?
12 What words and phrases does the judge use to explain why he did this and his problem in sentencing the man?

3

Summary

Use these short notes to summarise the main points in the magistrate's story.

1 the man/only just/out of prison
2 in a small town/everybody/everybody else
3 the man/very hard/get a job but nobody . . .
4 into a house/get some money
5 said/enough money/feed his family
6 I think/did it because/wanted to get caught
7 knew/in prison nobody would/down on him
8 wouldn't have/worry/money and food
9 if I/in his place/the same thing
10 I/back to prison

4

Discussion (and/or extended writing)

1 Imagine you are the man himself. Describe how you felt and why you broke into the house.
2 What do you think can be done with cases like this? Do you think that sending the man back to prison will help or harm the man? Give reasons.

David has an accident one evening.

1

Story

It was late. David was driving home. There was a cross roads ahead. Suddenly, a careless driver in another car turned into his path without signalling. David ran into him.

He jumped out and quickly looked at the damage. His front headlight had been smashed and the wing on the left side had been dented. The driver of the car had got out, too. He looked very angry. David politely suggested that they had better exchange names and addresses. But the other driver began shouting. "It was your fault!" he said furiously. Then he accused David of not paying attention and of driving dangerously. David was astounded. He looked around for witnesses. There was a woman standing on the corner. He asked her if she had seen the accident. She said she had.

The woman said it had not been David's fault but this only made the other man more furious. He went on arguing. Then David noticed that they were holding up the traffic. He suggested they should move their cars out of the way. The other man was still very angry but he got back into his car. He shook his fist at David, started the engine and then backed into a lorry that had stopped behind him.

2

Vocabulary

Find the words or phrases that mean these things.

1 where two roads meet
2 harm done in an accident, etc.
3 what happens to metal when it is struck hard
4 give each other something
5 show other drivers you are going to turn
6 very very surprised
7 people who see an accident
8 prevent traffic from moving
9 made an angry gesture with his hand

3

Questions

1 Describe how the accident happened.
2 Describe the damage to David's car.
3 What happened *before* the other driver began shouting?
4 What did he accuse David of?
5 Who was the witness? What did she say?
6 What did David suggest? Why?
7 Describe what happened then.

 Practice

4a

He accused David of { driving dangerously
not paying attention

Make more examples. Suppose the driver said:

1 "You caused the accident!"
2 "You were driving too fast."
3 "You weren't looking!"
4 "You didn't stop in time!"
5 "You're lying!"

4b

Transfer

A man and his wife had an argument. They said things like, "You don't love me!" and "You never talk to me!" etc. What did they accuse each other of doing? (Think of more examples!)

5a

David *suggested* that they *should* move their cars out of the way.

Make more examples. Suppose David said:

1 "Let's stop arguing."
2 "Let's find some witnesses."
3 "Let's tell the police."
4 "Let's discuss this calmly."
5 "Let's have a drink."

5b

Transfer

A man and his wife had an argument. Afterwards the man said things like: "Let's forget about it." and "Let's go to the cinema." What did he suggest they should do? (Make more examples.)

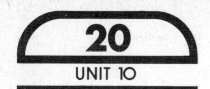

Listen to the dialogue. Then reproduce David's part.

1

Dialogue

DAVID: .... think .... names and addresses, ... we?

MAN: Look what you've done to my car!

DAVID: What *I* .... *your* car? Now .... moment!

MAN: No! *You* listen to *me*! It was your fault!

DAVID: *My* ....! .... mean?

MAN: I was signalling. You should've seen me. You were driving dangerously. You weren't paying attention.

DAVID: You weren't ....! And I wasn't ....!

MAN: You caused the accident! I didn't!

DAVID: I think .... better .... a witness! I mean, there must .... saw the accident!

David sees a woman on the corner

DAVID: Excuse .... Did .... the accident?

WOMAN: Yes, I did. I saw it very clearly.

DAVID: And .... see .... signalling?

WOMAN: No, I didn't. He wasn't signalling.

DAVID: I think .... better .... name and .... just in case I .... Could you .... to me?

WOMAN: Certainly! My name's Howard and ....

MAN: I was signalling! It was your fault!

Cars begin hooting

DAVID: Look! We're .... the traffic. Let's .... our cars .... the way!

MAN: All right! All right! But don't you try to get away.

The man gets into his car

WOMAN: Just look at him. He's so angry!

DAVID: Yes, ... certainly looks ...., ... he?

The man backs into a lorry behind him

DAVID: Now look .... what .... done! He .... into that .... behind ....!

Practice

2a

David suggested it was a good idea to exchange names and addresses. He said:

"I think we'd better exchange names and addresses, hadn't we?

Suppose he wants to suggest it is a good idea to:

1 look at the damage
2 tell the police
3 inform the insurance company
4 stop arguing
5 wait for the police
6 get off the road

2b

Transfer

You are a teacher in an evening school. Suggest to the class that it is a good idea to:

1 finish the lesson now
2 go home
3 do the next lesson
4 take a break
5 prepare for the test

What are some other examples of this pattern you might use in this situation?

2c

David did not say:

"I want to have your name and address. Perhaps I'll need them."

Instead he said:

 "I think I'*d better have* your name and address *just in case* I *need* them!"

Transform in the same way.

1 I want to borrow some money. Perhaps I'll need some.
2 I want to leave now. Perhaps the bus will come early.
3 I want to take this umbrella. Perhaps it will rain.
4 I want to study. Perhaps there'll be a test tomorrow.
5 I want to borrow your revolver. Perhaps someone will attack me.

2d

Transfer

You are going out. You say, "I'd better take an umbrella just in case it rains." What do you say if you think perhaps:

1 you'll need extra money
2 it'll get colder
3 you'll do some shopping

LOOK, SOUND, SMELL, FEEL, etc.

1a   Study this model.

	1	2
He	looks seems sounds appears	tired angry pleased
The coffee	smells	good
I	feel	awful

1b   Now read this.

1 We use verbs like this to describe what our senses (sight, hearing, smell, touch) tell us about something or someone.
Example: That coffee smells good.
These verbs have adjectives (see box 2 in the model) after them. Make more sentences with adjectives of your own that can go in box 2!

2 These verbs are generally used in the simple, and not the continuous; however *feel* and *look* can be used in both simple and continuous, without any real change in meaning.

1c   Now answer as B does, with *look, sound, smell* or *feel*

▌A: **Look at the man! He's so angry.**
▌B: **Yes, he certainly looks angry, doesn't he?**

1 Ah, they're making coffee in the next room. It must be good.
2 Listen to that man talking. He's stupid.
3 Sit on the bed. Isn't it hard?
4 Come and inspect the car. It's new.
5 Can you hear those children? They're very excited.
6 Can you see that man over there? He's very happy.

HAD BETTER

Comment **1d** ▌ **We'd (had) better exchange addresses.**

1 *Had better* is a modal verb. *Had* is *not* the auxiliary *had*, as in "They had left when I got there."
2 Note the *plain infinitive* form (We'd better *exchange* addresses).
3 It is often used to give advice, as in "You'd better see a doctor about that cough" or to make suggestions as in "I think we'd better find a witness".

EXTENDED WRITING
(and/or oral practice)

2   Work out either a short story or a conversation based on the following facts.

You are driving home one evening. You suddenly have to brake because another car in front of you stops without any warning at all. You do not run into the car in front but *a car behind* you runs into you. The driver is very angry and accuses you of stopping without warning. You try to explain about the car that was in front of you, which, in the meantime, has driven off. Finally, you find a witness who saw the whole thing and tells the driver of the car behind you that your story is true.

THE WORLD OF ADVERTISING

The EBC did a programme on advertisements. Here are some of them. Are they typical?

> Don't you want me to get that promotion? Don't you want my shirts to be whiter than anybody else's?

> Of course I do, darling. Please don't shout at me! It isn't my fault I can't get your shirts any whiter!

> I'd advise you to use GLEAM. It's so much better than ordinary washing powders!

> GLEAM

> I got that promotion yesterday, darling, and all because of you!

> (thinks) No, darling. All because of new MIRACLE GLEAM!

1

A few months ago, Mr and Mrs Smith had a big problem. He had a chance to get a promotion at work. Naturally, she wanted him to get it. And, like all good wives, she wanted him to look his best at all times and to make a really good impression at work. She worked very hard to make his clothes look clean. But in spite of all her hard work, she could never get his shirts as white as she wanted them to be.

Practice

a

Describe:
1 the chance he had
2 what she wanted him to do
3 their problem

b

Now use these words in questions beginning, "Did she want her husband . . . ?"
1 that promotion
2 his best at all times
3 a good impression at work
4 shirts that weren't really white
5 shout at her

2

Then, one day, a good friend happened to visit Mrs Smith. She told her how to solve the problem. "I'd advise you to use new, miracle GLEAM! It's so much better than ordinary washing powders!" she said.

Questions

Ask and answer:
1 who visited Mrs Smith
2 what she advised her to do
3 why

3

Mrs Smith took her friend's advice. Now Mr Smith's shirts are as white as he wants them to be, and his firm wants him to be their new sales director. And now Mrs Smith wants him to get an even better job. She wants him to become General Director! And she knows he can do it, with the help of GLEAM. "I should have used GLEAM before!" she says now.

Questions

Ask:
1 if Mrs Smith took the advice
2 what Mr Smith's shirts are like now
3 what his firm wants him to do
4 what Mrs Smith wants him to do
5 what she says now

Now read this advertisement. Then ask and answer questions about it.

4

Hello. My name's Bill Pepper. Only a few years ago, I was a weakling. My life was miserable. All the girls laughed at me. But then something happened that changed my whole life. Would you like me to tell you about it?

Questions

a

First, tell the whole story in this advertisement. Begin, "One day Bill was lying on the beach with . . . when . . ."

b

Ask questions about each picture like, "What is happening here?" "Why is Bill angry?" or "Why is he happy?" "What is . . . saying?"

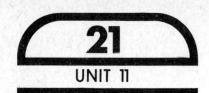

21
UNIT 11

1

Study the pattern.

She wanted him
{
to get a better job.
to buy some new shirts.
to give her a new washing machine.
}

Some of these verbs can go in place of *wanted*; some cannot. Which are they? Make sentences where possible!

> advised/suggested/begged/got/ordered/
> insisted/expected/told/asked/planned/hoped/
> allowed/demanded/permitted/forced/supposed

The answers
are in this
box, printed
upside down.

> permitted/forced
> expected/told/asked/allowed/
> advised/begged/got/ordered/

2a

Her friend
{
showed
told   her what to do.
advised
}

Make more sentences like this, with various verbs. For example, suppose Mrs Smith said: "What shall I do? Can you advise me?" Her friend could, and did. In other words: She advised her what to do. Now say what Mrs Smith's friend did if Mrs Smith said:

1 How can I get these shirts clean? Can you tell me?
2 How can I start this washing machine? Show me!
3 Which washing powder should I use? Can you advise me?
4 Where can I get it? Can you tell me?
5 What should I do? Show me!
6 How long should I keep the shirts in the machine? Tell me!
7 When should I take them out? Can you tell me?
8 How can I dry them? Show me!

2b

Transfer

An English friend is visiting you. Yesterday he went into town alone. You couldn't go with him. So you told him how to get there, what to say to the bus conductor, advised him what to do in town, etc. Make more sentences of your own.

 Would you like me to tell you how to become strong and manly?

3

Now imagine you are Bill Pepper. You want to tell people different things. You ask them various questions first about each situation, like this.

SITUATION: **You want to tell people about your body-building course.**
YOU ASK: *Would you like me to tell you about my body-building course?*

Think of more such questions beginning, *"Would you like me to . . ."*

1 You want to show them your muscles.
2 You want to tell them your secret.
3 You want to describe the body-building course.
4 You want to take off your shirt.
5 You want to lift three people into the air.
6 You want to show them where the body-building centre is.

In spite of/because of

4a

Make sentences with either *in spite of* or *because of*; like this.

> **They went out. The weather was bad.**
> *In spite of* **the bad weather, they went out.**
> **They didn't go out. The weather was bad.**
> **They didn't go out** *because of* **the bad weather.**

1 His work was good. He didn't get a promotion.
2 His work was good. He got a promotion.
3 Everybody admires him. He has talent.
4 Nobody admires him. He has talent.
5 The weather was wonderful. She stayed inside.
6 The price was low. Everybody bought it.
7 The price was low. Nobody bought it.

4b

Transfer

You like your job. You are telling someone this. You say things like: "I like my job because of . . . ." or "I like my job in spite of . . . ."

1 The hours are long.
2 The people are pleasant.
3 The pay is low.
4 The work is interesting.

Think of more things you might say!

5a

Comment

Should've been doing can be seen simply as *has/have been doing* or *was/were doing* combined with the idea of *should*. In the same way, *should've done* can be seen as *has/have done* or *did* combined with the idea of *should*.

Now answer as Robert Wilson does here.

> LINDA: **I haven't finished the report yet.**
> ROBERT: **Really? You should've finished it!**
> LINDA: **I've been working on something else.**
> ROBERT: **Really? You shouldn't have been working on something else!**

1 I haven't even started it.
2 I was taking a nap when you came in.
3 I've been using your phone.
4 I used it yesterday.
5 And I've been looking through your letters.
6 I've read them.
7 I was reading them when you came in.
8 I threw some of them away.

5b

Transfer

You work in an office. Yesterday the office manager was away, so you, two secretaries and the office boy used his office to have a party. The office manager came back in the middle of it. You weren't working. You were dancing. You didn't stop when he came in. You asked him if he wanted to dance, as well. Naturally, he was furious. Describe all the things you should have done, shouldn't have been doing, etc. Think of more examples!

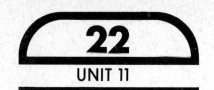

Intensive Listening

 An advertising man talks about his work.

1

Vocabulary

beauty soap: special soap for women.

complexion: smoothness, quality and colour of someone's skin.

define: say what something means.

advert: shortened form of "advertisement".

challenging: (here) requires a high standard of work.

life insurance: an arrangement with an insurance company. You pay a certain sum, and if you die before a certain age, the company gives your family a far larger sum.

providing for: taking care of.

get across an idea: (here) communicate an idea.

outline: lines showing a general shape.

caption: words or title explaining what a picture is about.

2

Questions (to be answered after you have listened to the tape)

1 According to the interviewer, something is often said about advertising. What?
2 What is the example that he gives?
3 Does the advertising man agree that advertising is a form of lying?
4 Why doesn't he enjoy writing adverts for things like beauty soaps?
5 What sort of advert did he have to do once that *was* challenging?
6 What can't you do in such adverts?
7 Why?
8 Describe the photograph in this advert.
9 How did he get over the idea that the husband was no longer there?
10 What did the caption say?

3

Summary

Use these short notes to summarise what you have just heard.

1 often said/advertising/lying
2 example/film star/a particular beauty soap every morning/but/never/at all
3 the advertising man/enjoy such adverts/not challenging enough
4 once/had to do/for life insurance
5 couldn't mention/death/because such things/unpleasant
6 so/got a family photograph of/in the park
7 then figure of the man/removed but/left the outline
8 still see where/been
9 top of the photograph/this caption: "We'll/care of them if anything/to you"

 Discussion (and/or extended writing)

4a

Describe an advertisement that tries to persuade people to buy something by saying a famous person uses it.
Then say whether you would buy the product yourself simply because of the advert. Give reasons.

4b

Describe the things adverts say about the following products in order to make you buy them:

1 cars
2 toothpaste
3 breakfast cereals like cornflakes, etc.
4 life insurance

If possible, get some English newspapers or magazines like the *Daily Mirror*, the *Daily Express*, or *Life*. Look at the advertisements in them for the products mentioned above.

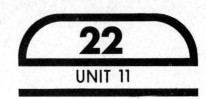

Linda has some trouble in a store.

1

Story

Linda was not satisfied. She had bought a sweater from a chain store and when she had washed it, the colour had run and the sweater itself had shrunk, even though she had followed the washing instructions exactly.

When she took it back, the salesgirl looked at it suspiciously. "You must have washed it in boiling water," she said. Linda told her she had used lukewarm water, just as the label said she should. Since the salesgirl still refused to exchange the sweater, Linda insisted on seeing the manager.

The manager was not very helpful, either. He did not want to admit that the sweater was not really washable. Suddenly Linda noticed a poster on the wall. It was an advertisement for the store. It said, "We give our customers satisfaction!" Linda pointed to it and asked if it really meant what it said. The manager looked embarrassed. Then he appeared to notice something. The sweater had a flaw. One of the threads was a different colour from the others. Then he said they would exchange the sweater after all. But he emphasised this was only because of the flaw. Linda stared but could not see the flaw. However, she smiled and said nothing. She had got what she wanted.

2

Vocabulary

Which words or phrases mean these things?

1 one store of many, all in the same firm
2 the colour had come out
3 it had got smaller
4 small ticket with name of maker, etc.
5 warm but not hot
6 give one thing in place of another
7 small mistake in material
8 thin piece of wool, cotton, etc.
9 say something very clearly and firmly

3

Questions

1 Why was Linda not satisfied?
2 What did the salesgirl say and do when Linda took the sweater back?
3 What did Linda do to get the manager?
4 What did the manager say at first?
5 What did he not want to admit?
6 What happened then?
7 Why did Linda "smile and say nothing"?

Practice

4a

■ **Linda insisted on seeing the manager.**

Make more such sentences. Suppose she said:

1 "I must have my money back!"
2 "I want to speak to the Company President."
3 "I must phone him immediately."
4 "I want to exchange it."
5 "I must eat some caviar for lunch!"

4b

Transfer

You are in England. The police arrested you yesterday. You said things like: "I must have a private cell, phone the Queen, be alone with my lawyer, and think about things for a while!" etc. What did you insist on? (Think of more examples!)

4c

Join these pairs, like this.

■ **Linda wanted something. She got this thing.**
Linda got what she wanted.

1 The manager said something. She understood.
2 The salesgirl said something. Linda disagreed with it.
3 Something was on the label. She had read it.
4 Linda had bought something. She was not satisfied with it.
5 The manager said something. She smiled at it.

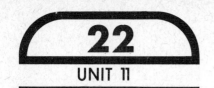

Dialogue/Practice

22

UNIT 11

Listen. Then reproduce Linda's part.

1

Dialogue

SALESGIRL: Yes, madam? May I help you?

LINDA: Yes, ... sweater. I .... here last month. A few days .... I .... it and the colour .... and the sweater ....

SALESGIRL: Hmm. You must have washed it in boiling water.

LINDA: No ....! I .... washing instructions! I .... it .... water, just as .... label ....

SALESGIRL: Well, I'm afraid I can't exchange it for you.

LINDA: ....? .... Well, ... see the manager.

SALESGIRL: I'm afraid he's busy.

LINDA: .... sorry but .... see him.

SALESGIRL: Very well. If you insist. One moment.

She goes for the manager

MANAGER: Yes, madam. May I help you?

LINDA: .... about this sweater. When I .... the colour .... and the sweater .... even though .... instructions ....

MANAGER: Really? This has never happened before.

LINDA: .... always .... first time, ... there?

MANAGER: I, er, I really don't see what we can do.

LINDA: Excuse .... but .... poster over ....?

MANAGER: Yes, what about it?

LINDA: ...., "We .... satisfaction."

MANAGER: Yes, I know what it says.

LINDA: Well, this store .... supposed .... satisfaction! But I .... satisfied.

MANAGER: I, uh, hmm. There's a flaw in this sweater. One of the threads is a different colour.

LINDA: ....? I can't ....

MANAGER: Yes, there's definitely a flaw there. All right, madam. We'll exchange it for you, but only because of the flaw.

Practice

2a

The salesgirl is sure Linda has washed the sweater in boiling water. She says:

■ **"You must have washed it in boiling water."**

What does she say to Linda if she is sure that Linda has:

1 bought it somewhere else
2 used the wrong kind of soap
3 had it for a long time
4 misunderstood the instructions
5 poured some kind of chemical on it

2b

Transfer

You have gone to meet a friend at a railway station. The train has just come in but he is not on it. You can only guess why, but you think he has probably:

1 come on another train
2 arrived at another station
3 taken a taxi
4 gone to your home
5 got lost

What do you say with *must have* ....? Think of more examples.

2c

The advertisement says, "We give satisfaction." In other words, we can say about the store:

■ **"It's *supposed to give* satisfaction."**

What do we say about:

1 a sweater; the label says "washable"
2 a man; people say he's very foolish
3 his wife; people say she beats him
4 they also say she goes out with other men
5 a film star; people say she's hard to work with
6 a pop star; people say he takes drugs

2d

Transfer

Think of famous people, certain countries and nationalities; what do people say about them? Make sentences with *supposed to* ....

Grammar Summary/Revision

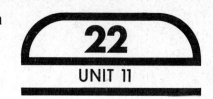

**WHAT
AS
SUBJECT
OR
OBJECT**

1a The subject or object of a sentence can be as simple as *it*; as in these two examples.

> **Subject**   **Object**
> ↓   ↓
> **It was interesting. I liked it.**

But we may wish to make a whole clause into the subject or the object of the sentence. One way of doing this is to use *what* clauses. They can be very complicated.

> **Subject**
> ⎴⎴⎴⎴⎴⎴⎴⎴⎴⎴⎴⎴⎴⎴⎴⎴⎴⎴⎴⎴⎴
> **What he said at the party yesterday**   was interesting.
>
> **Object**
> ⎴⎴⎴⎴⎴⎴⎴⎴⎴⎴⎴⎴⎴⎴⎴⎴⎴⎴⎴
> **I liked**   what he said at the party yesterday.

1b Make such sentences yourself, with the what-clause as the subject or the object, like this:

> **You said something to me. It was interesting.**
> **What you said to me was interesting.**
> **You said something to me. I didn't understand it.**
> **I didn't understand what you said to me.**

1 Your assistant said something. It was wrong.
2 Your assistant said something. I didn't hear it.
3 You are trying to do something. It is good.
4 You are trying to do something. I understand it.
5 We are doing something. It is not very easy.
6 We are doing something. We are trying to explain it.

1c These are more difficult.

1 I am saying something. Can you understand it?
2 He is holding something in his hand. Can you see it?
3 I am going to do something. It's unpleasant.
4 You said something to Mary at the party. It was very bad.
5 You said something to Mary at the party. It made her angry.
6 You wrote something to me in a letter a week ago. I've forgotten it.
7 You want to do something. Does everybody know it?

EXTENDED WRITING
(and/or oral practice)

2 You bought a gramophone record a few days ago. When you took it home you found there was a bad scratch on it. You took it back. The assistant refused to exchange it because she said you had made the scratch yourself. You insisted on seeing the manager. At first he refused to exchange the record, too. After an argument he finally gave in and exchanged it for you.

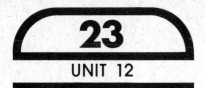

23
UNIT 12

Work and Money

1

I'm a pop star. I earn about £60,000 a year. Being a pop star means all sorts of things. It means I don't have to worry about money any more. It means I can do what I want to do. For example, I hate having to get up early. I can't stand working in offices or in factories. I can't bear having to work at fixed hours. That's why I enjoy being a pop star. I like playing in front of large audiences. I even like all those young girls screaming and trying to tear my clothes off.

Questions

Find questions and answers; like this. Find out about his job:
  Q: What sort of job does he do?
  A: He's a pop star

Now find out about:

1 the money he earns
2 if he has to worry about money
3 if he can do what he wants to do
4 the things he can't stand, hates, or can't bear doing
5 the things he likes or enjoys doing

(If you wish, make this into an imaginary interview. You are the interviewer and someone else in the class is the pop star.)

2

I'm a nurse and I don't earn very much money at all. In fact, I have a lot of difficulty in just making ends meet, as we say. But I like being a nurse. I suppose it's because I enjoy helping people. Being a nurse is hard work. It means working all sorts of hours. And it isn't very pleasant sometimes. There are all sorts of things I don't enjoy. For example, I don't enjoy seeing people in pain. Working ten hours a day and more in a hospital isn't much fun, but at least you know you're doing something worthwhile.

Questions

Ask and answer. Find out about:

1 this girl's job
2 the money she earns
3 if she can make ends meet
4 the things she likes doing or enjoys doing
5 if being a nurse is easy
6 the hours she works
7 if it's always pleasant
8 the things she does not enjoy
9 why she does this kind of work

3

I'm a policeman. Not many people like policemen. They say we're always stopping people from doing what they want to do. But I like my job. When I'm on holiday, I always look forward to getting back to work. A lot of my work is hard and boring. But in spite of the hard work, I still enjoy being a policeman. I'd never think of doing anything else.

Questions

Ask and answer. Find out:
1 how people feel about policemen
2 why they feel this way
3 how this policeman feels about his work
4 if he looks forward to getting back to work when he's on holiday
5 if his job is always interesting
6 if he enjoys it
7 if he would like to do something else

4

I'm a millionaire. In fact, I'm one of the richest men in the world. I can't say that I enjoy being so rich but I think I'd enjoy being poor even less. People say I'm not a very happy man. I don't suppose I am. I remember being happy only once in my life. That was just after I'd made my first million. I remember my wife saying, "Isn't life wonderful? We're rich!" Life isn't really so wonderful. Having money doesn't solve all your problems. But I don't mind having the problems as long as I've got the money, too.

Questions

Find out:
1 how rich this man is
2 if he enjoys it
3 how he would feel about being poor
4 if he is happy or can ever remember being so
5 what he remembers about that time in his life
6 if having money solves all your problems
7 if he minds having problems

5

Questions

There must be many things in your daily life that you hate, enjoy, can't stand or can't bear doing. What are they? (For example: talk about the crowded buses you have to travel in, the things you like or don't like doing at work or at school, etc.)

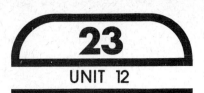

Remember/stop/enjoy/
mind . . . .ing

1

You are interviewing the millionaire. Ask various questions, like this.

> **He has met you before. Ask if he remembers.**
> **Do you remember meeting me?**

1 Once, he was very poor. Ask if he enjoyed it.
2 He worried about money. Ask when he stopped.
3 He is one of the richest men in the world. Ask if he enjoys it.
⁴ He gives interviews, but he can't stand it. Ask why.
5 He used to smoke big cigars. Ask when he stopped. Then ask why.
6 You want him to give another interview to-morrow. Ask if he would mind.

He hates having to get up early.

2a

Notice how these modals become gerunds.

> **He *has* to give interviews. He can't bear it.**
> **He can't bear *having* to give interviews.**
> **He *can* do anything he likes. He enjoys it.**
> **He enjoys *being able* to do anything he likes.**

Now you do it.

1 He has to sleep on trains. He does not enjoy it.
2 A long time ago, he had to work hard. He can remember it.
3 He can go on long holidays. He enjoys it.
4 He had to stay in cheap hotels a long time ago. He did not enjoy it.
5 He had to take orders from other people. He can still remember it.
6 He had to get up very early every morning. He could not bear it.

2b

Transfer

What are some of the things you enjoy being able to do or can't bear having to do?

She has difficulty in making ends meet.

3

Notice how verb phrases like *have difficulty in, have something against, look forward to* and *object to* take gerunds. Make examples, like this.

> **An old woman is trying to get across the street. She is having difficulty.**
> **She is having difficulty in getting across the street.**

1 The policeman will go back to work soon. He is looking forward to it.
2 The millionaire gives interviews but he has something against it.
3 Those students are going to take a test. They aren't looking forward to it.
4 That pop star is trying to get up. He is having difficulty.
5 I'm trying to concentrate and I'm having difficulty.
6 I'm going to have a rest and I'm looking forward to it.

Gerunds as subject clauses

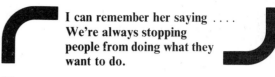

I can remember her saying . . . .
We're always stopping
people from doing what they
want to do.

4a

Notice how the nurse here talks about things without mentioning who does them.

> She works ten hours a day in a hospital. It isn't much fun.
> She says: **Working ten hours a day in a hospital isn't much fun.**

Make similar sentences yourself.

1 She helps doctors in the operating theatre. It's interesting.
2 She takes care of old people. It takes a lot of patience.
3 She sees people die. It isn't very pleasant.
4 She is a nurse in a large city hospital. This is very good experience.
5 She works long hours without a break. It is very tiring.
6 She does all these things. It is worthwhile.

4b

Transfer

Now talk about some of the things you do every day in the same way. Do not mention who does them. Say whether they are boring, interesting, tiring, etc. For example:

1 You study a foreign language. This takes a lot of time.
2 You work in a . . . . . It is very . . . . .
3 You listen to English radio programmes and read English papers. This is a good way to learn English.

5a

Note the form of the gerund subject

I can remember	her	doing it.
I object to	him	
I stopped	them	from doing it.
	you	

Now make sentences yourself, like this.

> *I* sat in the boss's chair. He objected to it.
> The boss objected to *me* sitting in his chair.

1 I smoked his cigars. He objected to it.
2 I kissed his secretary. He stopped me from doing it.
3 He shouted at me. I can remember it.
4 He hit me. I remember it.
5 The secretary screamed. I tried to stop her.
6 Then the police arrested me. But I don't remember it.
7 The boss says I hit him. He says he definitely remembers it.

5b

Transfer

Yesterday you happened to be in a bank when three men came in and robbed it. One of them hit you over the head. You are telling the police what you remember happening. You say things like, "I can remember the men coming in and . . ." etc. What else do you say to them? These are some of the things you remember:

1 The men told everybody to raise their hands. .
2 A woman screamed.
3 One of the men slapped her.
4 Another man took your money.

Now go on. What else do you remember happening?

Intensive Listening

24

UNIT 12

Three people talk about their jobs.

1

Vocabulary

frustrating: causing frustration.

survivors: those who live through a disaster or accident.

Head Office: the central office in a large firm.

dealing with: (here) working with.

in spite of that: even though.

give you a pretty free hand: they let you do what you want to do.

assembling: putting together.

assembly line: mass production technique where one person does one small job over and over again.

2

Questions (to be answered after you have listened to the tape)

2a

About the writer

1   What is the frustrating part of his job?
2   What are the things he enjoys doing?

2b

About Mr Griffin, the supermarket manager

1   What does the job involve?
2   What does he enjoy about it?
3   What does he say about taking orders from other people?
4   What does he say about "Head Office"?

2c

About the man on the assembly line

1   What sort of work does his job involve?
2   What are the things he looks forward to doing?
3   What's different about football?

3

Summary

Use these notes to reproduce parts of what each person said.

3a

The writer

1   being a writer/in front of a typewriter all day/ doesn't seem/real job/lot of people
2   lonely job/frustrating sometimes
3   but I enjoy/finished product
4   enjoy/in shops/my name on it
5   best part of my job/interesting people

3b

Mr Griffin

1   involves/with people/keeping them happy/to their problems
2   like the sense/responsibility
3   like/my own boss
4   don't like/orders from other people

3c

The man on the assembly line

1   my job/mostly assembling refrigerators
2   forward to/football on Sunday
3   completely different/my job because/never know/to expect

4

Discussion (and/or extended writing)

What would you like or dislike about each of these three jobs?

David has a bad tooth. He is at the dentist's.

1

Story

The tooth had been bothering David for some time. He knew he should have gone to the dentist's earlier. But in spite of the pain he had put it off. He always put off going to the dentist as long as possible.

The dentist smiled pleasantly at first. David told him that the tooth had kept him awake the night before. Then the dentist looked into his mouth, but he did not look only at the one tooth. Instead he looked them all over.

"Hmm," he said. "I'm afraid several of your teeth need seeing to." He smiled again. But this time it was a rather grim smile. He began to describe exactly what needed doing. David listened to him with a kind of sick feeling in his stomach.

"I should say that at least four teeth have cavities and then some of your old fillings are loose. We'll have to see to them immediately!"

David asked about the tooth that had been aching. "I may be able to save it," the dentist said, and smiled grimly again. He got his electric drill ready. "Now," he said with another grim smile, "this shouldn't hurt too much." He came nearer.

2

Vocabulary

Find the words or phrases that mean:

1 give trouble to
2 not do immediately
3 examine
4 hard; suggesting that something bad is about to happen
5 a kind of hole in teeth
6 what the dentist puts in the hole
7 take care of
8 dentist's instrument

3

Questions

1 Why had David gone to the dentist's?
2 What had he put off?
3 What was the first thing the dentist did?
4 What did he tell David?
5 What exactly was the work that needed doing?
6 What happened then?

Practice

4a

| David put off going to the dentist's. He should have gone earlier.

There are other things he should have done earlier and which he put off. What were they? He did not:

1 phone the dentist	4 get a haircut
2 pay his phone bill	5 pay his taxes
3 prepare next Tuesday's programme	6 book his holidays

4b

Transfer

You are going to take a test. You are thinking of all the things you put off doing and which you should have done earlier. What are they? For example:

1 you did not prepare for it
2 do the necessary homework
3 study the necessary books, etc.

Make more examples!

4c

Need doing is another way of saying *ought to be done*. Reply as B does here.

| A: **The dentist ought to see to those teeth.**
| B: **Yes, they really *need seeing* to, don't they?**

1 A mechanic ought to repair that car.
2 Somebody ought to look after those children.
3 The police ought to look into this matter.
4 Somebody ought to cut the grass.
5 You ought to clean this room.

24

UNIT 12

First, listen to the dialogue. Then use the skeleton to reproduce what David says.

1

Dialogue

DENTIST: What seems to be the trouble, Mr Nelson?
DAVID: .... tooth here. It's ....
DENTIST: I see. Has it given you a lot of trouble?
DAVID: .... awake last night.
DENTIST: Just let me have a look. Open wide, please (*looking into David's mouth*) Hmm. Now I'll just look over the other teeth.
DAVID: .... mean, you want .... over now? ·
DENTIST: Yes. Open wide, please. Now, when I press like this (*pressing*) ....
DAVID: Ouch!
DENTIST: Does that hurt?
DAVID: Yes, ...
DENTIST: Open again, please. Wider. And ... does *this* hurt?
DAVID: Yes, ... Which ....?
DENTIST: Just a moment, please. Open again. Hmm, I'm afraid several of your teeth need seeing to.
DAVID: ....? But .... only this one .... aching.
DENTIST: Yes, but in spite of that, I should say that at least four of your teeth have cavities.
DAVID: .... four ....? .... sure?
DENTIST: At least four, I should say. And then some of your old fillings are loose. Yes, hmm, four fillings will have to be seen to immediately.
DAVID: But what .... tooth .... been aching?
DENTIST: Oh yes. *That* one.
DAVID: .... think .... save it?
DENTIST: Well, I may be able to save it. Let's hope so. Now open wide, please. This shouldn't hurt too much.

 Practice

2a

What are the expressions here which you think almost any dentist would use before and while examining a patient?

2b

Respond as David does. Note the preposition and its position.

> DENTIST: **I'll just *look over* the other teeth.**
> DAVID: **You mean, you want to *look* them *over* now?**

1 I'll just take out this tooth.
2 I'll put in this filling
3 I'll fill in those cavities.
4 And then I'll pull out three teeth.
5 Let me take off my jacket.

2c

The dentist says that it is necessary to see to four fillings immediately. He says:

> **"Four fillings *will have to be seen to* immediately."**

In the same way, say that it is necessary to:
1 take an X-ray at once
2 pull out three teeth
3 do a lot of work today
4 see to a lot of things
5 put in four new fillings

2d

The dentist *isn't sure if he can* save the tooth but he *hopes to*. He says:

> **"Well, I *may be able to save* it."**

What do you say in the same situation if someone asks you:
1 Can you come to the party?
2 Can you do this work?
3 Can you learn all these words?
4 Can you repair the damage?
5 Can you carry this case?

Grammar Summary/Revision

PHRASAL VERBS
(Type 1)

1a Phrasal verbs are those that change their meaning in some way by the addition of one or more particles (prepositions or adverbs – words like *on, out, after, for*). For example, *give* changes its meaning completely when we say *give up a job*.

1b There are four basic types of phrasal verb. We are looking at *only one* type here. With phrasal verbs of type 1, when the object (*this jacket, those teeth*, etc.) is a *full noun* the particle may come either *before* or *after* it.

I'm going to	put	on	this jacket		put	this jacket	on
	give	up	that job	or	give	that job	up
	take	out	those teeth		take	those teeth	out

However, when the object is a *pronoun* (*it, them, you, him*, etc.) it *must* come *between* the verb and the particle.

I'm going to	put	it	on
	give	it	up
	take	them	out

This rule is true only of phrasal verbs of type 1!

1c Now answer as B does.

A: **I should put in these fillings.**
B: **All right, put in the fillings. Put them in now.**

1 I should take out those teeth now.
2 I should really turn off the light.
3 I'd better turn on the heating.
4 I'd like to give up my job.
5 I want to put off the appointment.

6 I'd like to ring up David Nelson.
7 I'd like to cut off my moustache.
8 We want to look over the audience figures.

EXTENDED WRITING
(and/or oral practice)

2 Write out this interview.

You are a television reporter. You are interviewing the pop star on page 96. (His name, by the way, is "Hot Lips Daniels".) Interview him about his likes and dislikes and the way he spends a typical day (what time he gets up, what he has for breakfast, what he does in the afternoon, when he goes to work, a typical concert, etc.) This interview should be about 200 words.

Women's Liberation

1

Read this article from a newspaper.

Women wish they had been born men

Sociologists working in Western European countries, especially West Germany and England, have found that a large number of women wish they had been born men. The number is said to be as high as 60% in West Germany.

"Women often wish they had the same opportunities that men have, and are convinced it is still 'a man's world'", said Dr James Holden, one of the sociologists who did the study.

Questions

Ask and answer.
You are talking to Dr Holden; you want to know:
1 what some women wish
2 why they wish they were men
3 how many wish they were men
4 in which countries

2

Anne Harper has a very responsible job for an international oil company. She also believes in "Women's Liberation". "I don't wish I were a man," she says, "and I don't think many women do. But I do wish people would stop treating us like second-class citizens. At work, for example, we often do the same job that men do but get paid less. There are still a lot of jobs . . . usually the best ones . . . that are open only to men. If you're a man you have a much better chance of leading an exciting life. How many women pilots are there . . . or engineers . . . or architects?"

Questions

Find out:
1 what sort of job Anne has
2 if she believes in "Women's Lib"
3 if she wishes she were a man
4 if she thinks many women do
5 what she wishes would happen
6 what she means by "second-class citizens"
7 what sorts of jobs are open only to men

Give the answers as well.

3

Barry Wood is a teacher. His wife is a computer programmer. Her job takes her out in the evenings a lot, and he often has to take care of the children. "Sometimes I wish I'd never said she could go out to work. I mean, I wish she would stay at home and look after the children. After all, that's a woman's job, isn't it? I wish I earned a bit more money. Then we could get along on my salary. But she says she'd still go out to work even if I had a better job. I just don't understand."

Questions

Find out:
1 what Barry's wife does
2 if he often takes care of the children
3 what he wishes his wife would do
4 why
5 why he wishes he earned a bit more money
6 if his wife would stay at home then
Give the answers as well.

Study this list of jobs. Some of them are said to be "a man's job"; others "a woman's job". Which are said to be which? Then give your own opinion.

bus driver   lorry driver   nurse   cook
bank manager   secretary   typist
professional footballer   garage mechanic
babysitter   train driver   beauty expert

Would people be surprised if they saw a man doing some of these jobs? Or a woman doing them? Why?

Would you be surprised if you heard a woman saying, "Sometimes I wish I were a . . ."? Make sentences like this that might be surprising for a man or a woman.

I wish my wife *would* stay at home.

I don't wish I *were* a man
I wish I *earned* a bit
more money.

1a

This pattern is often used when you want something to happen in the future. Study this situation.
Situation: The people in the flat above Linda are having a wild party. Linda is getting rather angry. She would like them to stop making so much noise. She says to herself:

■ **"I wish they'd stop making so much noise!"**

What does she say if she would like them to:

1 turn down the radio
2 keep their voices down
3 have their parties somewhere else
4 stop slamming doors
5 be a bit quieter
6 let her get some sleep

1b

Transfer

You are standing on a cold, windy platform, waiting for a train. What do you say if:

1 the train has not come yet
2 some people are pushing and shoving
3 it is raining

Think of other things you might say in:

1 a restaurant where the service is slow
2 a lecture hall where you can hardly hear the lecturer

2a

Comment

1 *Wish* and *were/did*, etc., is often used to talk about things people are dissatisfied with in the present.
2 The verb form after *wish* is the same as the simple past. Only *be* is different. Many people use *were* for all persons. Now study this situation.

2b

Situation: Barry Wood (the teacher whose wife goes out to work) is sorry that he *is* not rich.
He says, "I wish I were rich."
What does he say if he is sorry that:

1 he hasn't a better job
2 he doesn't live in a bigger house
3 he can't persuade his wife to stay at home
4 the child is not grown up
5 teachers' salaries are not higher
6 he doesn't know how to deal with children

2c

Transfer

A woman is very dissatisfied with the house she lives in and other things. What does she say about:

1 the house itself
2 the garden
3 the family car
4 her husband's job (it is not very good)
5 her figure (she is getting fat)

**Some women wish they
had been born men.
Barry wishes he *had* never
said his wife could go out
to work.**

3a

Comment

This pattern is often used when something happened in the past that you are sorry about. Study this situation.

Situation: A woman is arguing with her husband. She is sorry she ever met him.

▌ **She says: "I wish I'*d* never *met* you!"**

What does she say to him if she is sorry that she ever:

1 saw him
2 ran away with him
3 listened to his promises
4 married him
5 fell in love
6 left home
7 gave up her career
8 stopped teaching
9 came to London

3b

Transfer

There must be things you wish you'd never done or wish you had done (but didn't). What are some of them?

A young married woman is interviewed about her feelings towards "Women's Lib".

1

Vocabulary

militant: extremist, believer in strong, combative, fighting action.

burn your bra: ("bra" short for "brassiere", woman's underclothes). Women's Lib members sometimes do this to show their desire to be free of the restrictions imposed on women.

alluring: attractive, fascinating in a way.

threatened: ("He feels threatened.") (here) to feel that one is in a very dangerous position, that one's rights or status may be taken away.

redundant: unnecessary, extra to what is needed to do a job. Workers who, when new machines are introduced that do their work, lose their jobs are "declared redundant".

provide jointly for their family: (here) to work together (man and wife) to take care of the money needs of their family.

reared: brought up, as in, "Children are usually reared in families."

pushed into a role: (here) forced to play a part in life that they (women) do not want to play.

2

Questions (to be answered after you have listened to the tape)

1 In what way is this young woman different from some extreme militants in Women's Lib? What are the things she enjoys about being a woman?
2 What does she think women should be allowed to do?
3 She describes a man. What does his wife want to do?
4 How does he feel about this?
5 What does he want?
6 What will probably happen if his wife goes out to work?
7 Why will he perhaps feel "redundant"?
8 What does she think men and women ought to do in marriage?
9 She says "it's very unfortunate to see children" in a particular type of situation. Describe this situation.
10 In what way are the pressures of Women's Lib affecting women?

3

Summary

Use these short notes to summarise what the young woman says about herself and Women's Lib.

1 she enjoys/ woman.
2 thinks/ extremists in any movement but/ not one herself.
3 thinks/ fun/ woman/ pretty clothes/ alluring.
4 women/ allowed/ any job.
5 knows one man/ wife/ go out and earn money.
6 he/ wife sitting at home/ children/ toys put away.
7 if/ out to work he/ disorganised house.
8 feel threatened because/ whole way of life/ providing/ family.
9 redundant.
10 great possibilities/ men and women/ provide jointly.
11 unfortunate/ children being reared/ families/ mother bored and frustrated.
12 pressures of Women's Lib/ affecting women.
13 beginning to wonder/ pushed into a role/ really don't want.

4

Discussion (and/or extended writing)

1 Do you think there are any good arguments that can be put forward for the man described in the example the young woman gives? What are these arguments?
2 What about the woman? Think of arguments she might use.
3 Work out a dialogue between the two (man and wife) when things have finally come to a head and the man wants to forbid his wife to go out. What would he say about:
   (a) how his own work is suffering
   (b) his "rights" as a husband
   What would she say about:
   (a) the boring, frustrating life she leads at home
   (b) what can be done with the extra money she is earning

Story/Dialogue

1

Story

Linda had to go to Brighton one evening. She decided she would rather take a train than go by car. But when she got to the station, she found that only half the trains were running. Some of the drivers had gone on strike.

Linda wondered if there was any point in waiting. Just then she saw Margaret Dickinson. She was going to Brighton, too. "Come on. We'll push through the crowd," she said.

A long queue was waiting in front of the gate for the Brighton train. They joined it. They talked about the strike. "It's time we women went on strike, too. At the EBC, I mean," Margaret said. "They think they can pay us less because we're women. We have to get equal rights in pay and everything. We have to be treated exactly the same as men are! Exactly the same!"

Just then the gate was opened. Everybody began to push. The queue became a wild crowd. A man next to them pushed Margaret aside and got in front.

"There aren't any gentlemen left any more. Men don't even know how to treat a woman like a lady any more!" Margaret said loudly.

2

Vocabulary

Find the words or phrases that mean:
1 prefer to
2 refuse to work
3 number of people waiting in line
4 kind of metal fence in front of a platform
5 *the same* rights
6 push someone *out of the way*

3

Questions

1 What was the trouble at the station?
2 What did Linda wonder?
3 What did she and Margaret talk about?
4 What were some of the things Margaret said about women?
5 What happened when the gate opened?
6 Why did Margaret get angry?

(Practice)

4a

> She decided she would rather *take* a train than *go* by car.

Make more sentences beginning:
"She decided she would rather . . . than . . ."
Suppose she decided to:

1 take a taxi and not go by train
2 stay at home and not go to Brighton
3 have a cup of coffee; not wait there
4 see a film; not visit her friends

4b

Transfer

Choose one of these pairs. Say:

> "I think I'd rather . . . than . . . this evening."

This evening you can:
1 stay at home or go out
2 go dancing or play chess
3 do more homework or watch television
4 have an English lesson or see a film

4c

> She wondered if there was any point in waiting.

Make more such sentences. Suppose she did not know whether to:

1 stay there
2 join the queue
3 try to get a train
4 ask for more information
5 argue with Margaret

4d

Transfer

You have just woken up. It is Monday. You feel terrible. What are some of the things you might say beginning:
"I wonder if there is any point . . ."

26
UNIT 13

Dialogue/Practice

Listen to the dialogue on tape.
Then use the skeleton to reproduce what
Linda says.

1

LINDA: ...., ... which platform .... next Brighton train .... from?

GUARD: Platform 7, if you're lucky.

LINDA: .... lucky? .... understand.

GUARD: Half the trains aren't running. Some of the drivers are on strike again.

LINDA: .... no! .... point .... waiting?

GUARD: Can't tell you, I'm afraid.

Margaret suddenly comes by

MARGARET: Linda! What are you doing here?

LINDA: Oh, ... I'm .... Brighton.

MARGARET: So am I. Look! That's a Brighton train. Platform 7.

LINDA: Yes, but .... queue!

MARGARET: Yes, but what's the use of just looking at it? Let's get into it.

They join the queue

LINDA: .... strikes! .... so much trouble!

MARGARET: What else can the train drivers do? We could learn something from them.

LINDA: Learn ....? What .... mean?

MARGARET: I mean it's time we went on strike, too. The women at the EBC, I mean.

LINDA: .... so?

MARGARET: Don't *you* think we ought to get equal pay?

LINDA: Of course I ...., if .... same work.

MARGARET: They think they can pay us less because we're women.

LINDA: You mean, ... equal rights?

MARGARET: Exactly! We have to be treated exactly the same as men are. Exactly the same!

LINDA: ....! .... gate now!

MARGARET: Good lord. Just look at this crowd.

LINDA: .... pushing, ... in front!

MARGARET: Just look at that! That man! Pushing women aside!

LINDA: .... gentlemen .... more!

MARGARET: Exactly! They don't even know how to treat a woman like a lady!

Practice

2a

Margaret thinks it is foolish to just look at the queue. She says:

■ **What's the use of just looking at it?**

What does she say if she thinks it is foolish to:
1 stand here
2 talk about it
3 complain
4 get angry
5 try to get on such a crowded train
6 push and shove

2b

Transfer

You are an unhappy language student. You don't think you are learning anything. What are some of the things you might say beginning, "What's the use ...?"
For example:
1 try to learn
2 do language drills
3 sit in class all day, etc.

2c

Margaret says the women at EBC ought to *go* on strike, too. She says:

■ **It's time we *went* on strike, too.**

What does she say if she thinks:
1 everybody ought to get a rise
2 salaries ought to go up
3 the guard ought to open the gate
4 the train ought to leave
5 the police ought to do something about these strikes

2d

Transfer

A rather old-fashioned father is talking to his twenty-one year old son. What might he say if he thinks his son ought to
get a haircut, find a job, etc. (think of more examples!)

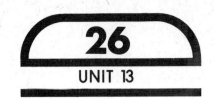
PHRASAL VERBS
(Type 2)

1a The second type of phrasal verb (see unit 12 for type 1) consists of:

verb	particle	preposition	
he put	up	with	it

Comments

1 The particle and the preposition are never separated from the stem (except with the verb *to be* used in the negative, as in number 7 below).

2 We have already seen various examples of this type in previous units.

1b Here are some examples of such verbs. They are on the left. See if you can match them with their meanings. Each example corresponds roughly in meaning to a verb on the right.

1 My friend Janet had always *looked up to* her boss.

2 She always *gave in to* his demands.

3 Then, one day, he *went back on* a promise.

4 He had promised to *get rid of* her old typewriter.

5 Then he suddenly said she would have to *put up with* it a bit longer.

6 She argued, but could not *get through to* him.

7 She said the old machine *was* not *up to* the job.

8 He got angry and shouted at her, but she *stood up to* him.

9 That was how she *fell out with* him.

10 Now she had decided to *put in for* a transfer to another department.

tolerate, not complain about;

apply for, try to get;

broke, did not keep;

agree to do something even though she did not always want to;

had great respect for;

could not do, did not have the necessary qualities for;

became unfriendly with;

throw away, replace;

communicate with;

fight, not run away from

EXTENDED WRITING
(and/or oral practice)

2 Do one of the following:

1 Barry Wood and his wife are arguing. He thinks she ought to stay at home. He cannot do his own work properly because she is out every evening on computer work. He cannot take care of the children and study for higher qualifications. She thinks she has a right to a career, too. (This should be in dialogue form.)

2 An essay between 200 and 300 words on the theme "Is it still a man's world?"

INFLATION

This is from a programme the EBC recently did on inflation.

2

Jean MacPherson is a teacher. She is giving a lesson to a class of more than thirty children. She has this to say: "Teachers don't go on strike. At least, the teachers in my school never have. But we want a better standard of living, too. I simply can't make ends meet any more. I can't afford new clothes. I can't even afford to have my old ones cleaned."

Questions

Ask and answer questions about Jean MacPherson. Find out:

1 what she is doing at the moment
2 if teachers go on strike
3 what teachers want
4 if she can make ends meet
5 what she can't afford

1

These men are on strike. They are striking for higher wages. They were given a rise last year but prices have gone up in the meantime. The rise has been wiped out by inflation.

Some of these men are shouting things like: "Give us more money. Give it to us now!" An offer was made to them yesterday by their employer but it was not good enough. It was rejected by them. But even if a better offer is made to them, it will be wiped out by inflation, too.

Questions

1 these men want something; ask what
2 they were given a rise; ask when
3 something has happened to prices in the meantime; ask what
4 something has happened to their rise; ask what
5 they are shouting something; ask what
6 an offer was made to them; ask when
7 it was rejected by them; ask why
8 something will happen to their next rise; ask what

Give the answers as well.

These newspaper cuttings illustrate other aspects of inflation, its causes and its results.

Union rejects latest pay offer

3 The British Railworkers Union rejected the latest English Railways offer of 8% today. One of their heads described the offer to one of our reporters as "ridiculous".

"Nothing under 10% will do. We've explained the position to English Railways time and time again," he said.

The head of English Railways, Robert Rivers, replied, "The union has been given a good offer. We can't do any better. This has been explained to the union again and again." The real problem is inflation. The railways cannot increase the offer without increasing rail fares. Rivers said, "We have a duty to fight inflation. So has the union."

Questions

a

1 Why did the union reject the offer?
2 What did one of their heads say?
3 How did he describe the offer?
4 What exactly did the head of English Railways say?
5 Why can't he increase the offer?

b

Now imagine you are interviewing the union man. Ask him:

1 to explain to you why he doesn't like the offer
2 to describe to you his men's feelings about the offer

c

Now interview Rivers. Ask him:

1 to explain to you why he can't increase the offer
2 to describe to you how he feels about inflation

Food prices go up again

4 Food prices went up by as much as 3% last month. Beef and other meat went up even more. Yesterday butchers were given a sharp warning by the Minister of Agriculture, Mr George Last. "Don't be greedy!" he told them.

Questions

1 What happened last month?
2 What were butchers given yesterday?
3 What exactly were they told and by whom?

Shoppers organise strike

5 "Housewives are always given a bad deal. It's time we did something about it!" These were the fighting words of Mrs Jane Ashby, who lives in the London suburb of New Eldon. "Everybody else gets more and more money. But we don't. Housewives should refuse to buy at certain shops. I'm organising a shoppers' strike and I've been told by all the housewives here that they'll support it," she said.

Questions

1 What exactly were the "fighting words" of Mrs Ashby?
2 What does she think housewives should do?
3 Why does she think she will get support for her strike?

27

UNIT 14

```
          1    2    3
Give/us/higher/wages!
          1    2    3
Give/them/to us/now!
```

They were given a rise.

1a

Comment

In the first sentence, *us* is called the *indirect object* and *higher wages* is called the *direct object*.

Question: What about the second sentence? Which words are the indirect object? Which words are the direct object?

1b

Invention exercise

Here are the most common verbs with which the two arrangements are possible. For each, make a pair of sentences. Think of the direct object and the indirect object yourself. Like this:

write: **Please write me a letter.**
 Write it to me soon!

teach/sell/bring/take/lend/send/hand/pay/
show/tell/pass

```
          1            2            3
We've explained/the position/to them.
```

2

There are a few verbs in English with which this is the only possible arrangement. The indirect object must have the preposition *to*, and the direct object usually comes first. Some of the most common of these verbs are given in column A. Can you make sentences with them by combining them with words in columns B and C?

A	B	C
explain	"good morning"	to us
describe	the accident	to your father
mention	the classroom	to the police
report	my name	to me
introduce	a solution	
suggest	the problem	
say	that pretty girl	

3

Observe that there are two possible passive forms with verbs like *give*.

 They were given a rise.
Someone gave them a rise.
 A rise was given to them.

Transform in the same way, using both forms.

1 Someone gave her £5,000.
2 Someone left her a lot of money.
3 Someone offered him a good job.
4 Someone lent him a million dollars.
5 Someone sent me this telegram.
6 Someone gave us this information.
7 Someone sold him London Bridge.
8 Someone told him this stupid story.

This has been explained to the union again and again.

4

This is the only possible passive form with verbs like *explain*. Make examples of your own.

Situation: Someone asks you to do something, but it has already been done. (Perhaps not by you, but it doesn't matter.)

> OTHER PERSON: **You ought to explain this to the union.**
>
> YOU: **It's already been explained to them!**

1 You ought to explain this to the class!
2 You ought to report the accident to the police.
3 Describe the thief to them!
4 Look at that pretty girl! Introduce her to me!
5 Mention my name to her!
6 I can't find the answer to this question. Couldn't you even suggest it to me?

1   2   3
I can't afford to have/my old clothes/cleaned.

5a

Comment

1 *Have something done* indicates that the thing is done by someone else.
2 Observe that in this construction the object (*my old clothes*) always comes between *have* and the participle (*cleaned, done*, etc.).

5b

Now see if you can do this substitution exercise.

I can't afford to have/these things/cleaned.

> **I'm going to have:** *I'm going to have* **these things cleaned.**
> **repaired: I'm going to have these things** *repaired*.
> **the brakes: I'm going to have** *the brakes* **repaired.**
> **I've just had:** *I've just had* **the brakes repaired.**

I can't afford to have these things cleaned.

1 all these clothes		7 When did you have
2 I've just had		8 the car
3 this suit		9 Where
4 I'm going to have		10 that dress
5 mended		11 made
6 the typewriter		12 She had

5c

Transfer

A young woman has just married a rich old man. He lives in a huge but very old-fashioned house. She wants a lot of changes to be made. Naturally, she is not going to do the work herself. She says things like:

> **"We really must have the house redecorated."**

and

> **"I'd like to have the garden redesigned."**

Make sentences for her. The changes involve:

1 decorating the bedrooms
2 building a new garage
3 painting the house pink
4 putting in a new toilet and bath
5 installing a new cooker
6 painting the kitchen white
7 cutting down five trees in the garden
8 planting some new trees
9 cutting the grass
10 repairing the garden gate

Intensive Listening

1

Vocabulary

wage inflation: inflation caused by higher and higher wages.

getting ahead a bit: making some progress; (here) improving one's standing of living a bit.

lose value: go down in worth or value.

the rate of inflation: the amount by which inflation increases.

accelerate: speed up, go faster.

lose confidence in: lose trust or belief in.

This is what I take . . . to be: this is what I think . . . is.

2

Questions (to be answered after you have heard the tape)

2a *The teacher from Scotland*

1 In what sense is inflation "depressing"?
2 What do some people say the cause of inflation is? How exactly does the interviewer explain it?
3 What does the teacher think is the cause?

2b *Mr Griffin*

1 How much was Mr Griffin earning a few years ago?
2 What did he think at the time?
3 How much is he earning now?
4 What does he think now?
5 What does he say about money?

2c *The economist*

1 What is the first question and what is the economist's answer?
2 Why is it difficult to say what the effects of inflation are?
3 What does he think is the main effect?

2d *The student*

1 What do you think the student means by "a terrible job"?
2 What does he mean by "the least you can expect" here?
3 What is his answer when he is asked, "What's a reasonable amount of money?"?
4 How does he describe the process that causes inflation?

3

Summary

Use these short notes to summarise some of the things that were said.

3a *The teacher*

1 all very depressing
2 a rise one month/wiped out/next
3 the more prices/up/the more/wages
4 unions always/more money

3b *Mr Griffin*

1 a few years ago/a bit of progress
2 £2,000 a year/ahead a bit
3 but now/£3,000/any better off
4 money/value

3c *The economist*

1 the rate of inflation/accelerating
2 the pound in your pocket/less and less
3 difficult/pick out one effect in particular because/so many
4 but/ most obvious one/ people/ confidence/ money

3d *The student*

1 if/a terrible job/the least you can expect/a reasonable amount of money for it
2 when/other people/more money for less work/ people will always want . . . .
3 one group of workers/wage increase/then another/and another
4 in order/increase wages/prices
5 when prices/people/more money again

4

Discussion (and/or extended writing)

Describe what you think happens in a time of inflation to:

1 old people on fixed pensions.
2 people like nurses who cannot go on strike.
3 young people who are just starting their careers and are trying to save up money in order to get married.

Margaret Dickinson has a simple job done to her car at a garage.

1

Story

The engine of Margaret's car was not running smoothly. The spark plugs needed cleaning; that was all. Margaret could have done the job herself, but garages have special equipment that does such things very thoroughly.

Margaret took after her father; she did not like being overcharged. She knew that garages do this sometimes. Sometimes they even charge for work they have never done. She told the mechanic at the garage not to do any extra work, she wanted the spark plugs cleaned, and nothing more. Then she left, saying she would be back in a little while.

When Margaret came back, the cashier handed her a bill for £1. Margaret knew this was more than it should cost to have the spark plugs cleaned. Then the cashier said they had put new ones in. Margaret decided she was not going to stand for this, and began to get angry.

"But the plugs were worn out; what else could we do?" the cashier protested. "How long should these new spark plugs last? More than a few months?" Margaret demanded. "Of course! Much longer than that!" the cashier said with great emphasis.

"Well, then, put the old ones back in. I had new spark plugs put in only a few months ago, and I had the job done here!" Margaret said.

2

Vocabulary

Find the words or phrases that mean:

1 going well, without difficulty
2 small part of engine that ignites petrol
3 resemble
4 ask for too high a price
5 paper showing how much money must be paid
6 put up with; allow
7 stress or force put on words to give them importance

3

Questions

1 What was wrong with Margaret's car?
2 Why didn't she do the job herself?
3 In what way did she take after her father?
4 What did she tell the mechanic?
5 What happened when she came back?
6 Why did she blow up?
7 What did the cashier say about the old plugs?
8 Describe what happened then.
9 What did Margaret tell the cashier to do, and why?

 Practice

4a

▌ She left, *saying* she would be back later.

Make more sentences like this.

1 Ten people stood there. They were waiting for the bus.
2 The bus drove up. It made a lot of noise.
3 It drove off. It splashed mud all over me.
4 I stood there. I shouted at the driver.
5 The driver stared at me. He forgot about the traffic.
6 A lorry ran into the bus. It killed the driver and ten people.
7 I stood there. I gaped.

4b

▌ She told him *not* to do any extra work.

Make more examples. Suppose her exact words were:

1 "Don't put any new plugs in!"
2 "Don't change the oil!"
3 "Don't spend too long on it!"
4 "Don't get the car dirty!"

5

Transfer

Yesterday Robert Wilson went to see a doctor. His health was poor because he was doing all sorts of things he should not do. What do you think the doctor told him not to do?

117

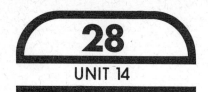

Dialogue/Practice

Listen. Then take Margaret's part.

1

Dialogue

MARGARET: The engine .... smoothly. I'd like .... at it.

MECHANIC: You want the engine looked at. All right.

MARGARET: No! I mean, ... the trouble is. The .... cleaning. .... all.

MECHANIC: All right. I'll see to it.

MARGARET: I .... plugs .... That's .... clear?

MECHANIC: Spark plugs. All right.

MARGARET: .... extra work without .... first.

MECHANIC: Yeah. Just leave it with us.

MARGARET: How much .... cost? To ...., I mean.

MECHANIC: Don't know. Not much.

MARGARET: Well, ... know. Could .... exact?

MECHANIC: About 30p, I suppose.

MARGARET: 30p. All right. I .... back .... while.

Margaret leaves. She comes back later

MARGARET: I .... car. .... Dickinson.

CASHIER: Dickinson. Oh, yes. The blue mini. That'll be £1, please.

MARGARET: ....? .... sure? £1 .... cleaned?

CASHIER: Ah, but you see, the old plugs were worn out so we put new ones in.

MARGARET: But .... only wanted .... cleaned! I didn't .... extra work ....!

CASHIER: But the plugs were worn out. What else could we do?

MARGARET: .... out? .... sure?

CASHIER: Yes! They were definitely worn out!

MARGARET: .... me. How long .... last? More .... a few months?

CASHIER: Of course! Much longer than that!

MARGARET: Well, ... Put .... back!

CASHIER: You want the old ones put back?

MARGARET: Yes! I had .... last month! And, ... more, I .... job .... here!

Practice

2a

"**How much should it cost? To have the spark plugs cleaned, I mean.**"

In the same way, ask about the cost of:
1 washing the car
2 testing the brakes
3 checking the steering
4 putting in a new engine
5 doing a new paint job
6 putting in a radio

2b

Transfer

First, ask similar questions with, "How long will it take ....?" and "Why does it cost so much ....?" Then work out similar questions you might ask:
1 in a shop where clothes are cleaned
2 if you want to have your house redecorated
3 in the office of a company that ships things by air and by rail

2c

Respond as B does, leaving out *to have*:

A: **I'd like someone to look at the engine.**
B: **You want the engine looked at. All right.**

Now suppose A says, "I'd like someone to ...."
1 take this to the post office
2 do a few small jobs
3 see to my typewriter
4 repair this watch
5 move the piano
6 take away all this rubbish

2d

Transfer

You are in a luxury hotel. You want someone to take your luggage to your room. You say, "I'd like this luggage taken to my room, please." In the same way, say you want someone to:
1 deliver some flowers
2 serve breakfast in bed
3 scrub your back

Think of more examples!

Grammar Summary/Revision

28

UNIT 14

PHRASAL VERBS
(Type 3)

1a These, like type 1 (see unit 12) have a verb and a particle.

verb   particle

I'll { look   after
see   to   } something
go   into   it

Comment 1b   **1** We call *to*, *after*, *into* particles and not prepositions here because their function with phrasal verbs is very different. Compare *go into* (examine) with *go into* (enter).

> **"Let's *go into* the problem deeply."**
> **"Let's *go into* the dining room."**

In which of the two examples is *go into* a phrasal verb?
In which of the two is *into* a true preposition?

2 Type 3 phrasal verbs are different from type 1 in one important respect. Type 3 phrasal verbs *never* separate the particle from the stem! The exercise illustrates this.

1c Replace the full noun in each sentence with a pronoun. (For example, *my father* becomes *him*.)

> **Type 3**   I looked *after* my father.→I looked *after* him.
> **Type 1**   I turned *on* the light.————→I turned it *on*.

1 I turned off the gas.
2 We went into the problem.
3 I put in the new spark plug.
4 I put off the appointment.   .
5 She looked after her old mother.

6 I ran into my friend at the night-club.
7 I won't stand for this nonsense.
8 I can't do without tobacco.
9 He gave up his job.
10 She took after her father.

EXTENDED WRITING
(and/or oral practice)

2a Write either a short story or a dialogue based on the following facts.

1 You took your car to a garage last week. One of the tyres needed changing. You told the mechanic there to change only one tyre.

2 When you came back the cashier handed you a bill for over £10. She calmly told you that *two* tyres were worn out, and that they had changed them both.

3 You were sure the other tyre was not worn out because you bought three new tyres only three months ago. You bought them at the same garage and had them put on there.

2b The garage you went to is only one of a national chain. The chain is called Pedley National Garages. Their address is: 12 St Christopher Square, London W.C.2.

Write a letter to the managing director. Describe exactly what happened and complain about this attempt to overcharge you. Remind the managing director that in these times of inflation everybody has a duty to keep prices down to a reasonable level and to give customers a "fair deal".

1

This was a part of London almost 100 years ago. Life must have been pretty terrible for the people in these houses. They had to put up with noise, smoke and dirt. The noise came from the railway, and the smoke and the dirt came from the trains and the thousands of chimneys all around them. The smoke often mixed with fog and hung in the air for days. Disease killed thousands of children. Families were large but often five out of seven children would die before they were five years old.

Questions

You are interviewing a historian.
Find out:

1 what people had to put up with 100 years ago in London
2 where the noise came from
3 where the smoke and dirt came from
4 how long the smoke hung in the air
5 why
6 if disease was a very great problem
7 if many children died before they were five

Give the answers as well.

2

Is life really better than it was 100 years ago? It is certainly true that people live longer than they used to, travel faster than they could and own more things than they did. We have made great progress in industry, science and medicine. But we still have to put up with noise, overcrowding and bad air. They are still a basic part of modern life.

Questions

1 In what ways is life better than it was?
2 What have we made progress in?
3 What do we still have to put up with?

Discussion

Are there any ways in which you think life is better for the people in the houses in the second picture than it was for those in the first? Describe these "improvements".

3

100 years ago there was a clear difference between town and country. But the motor car has changed all that. Motorways eat into the countryside. One motorway can take up an amazing amount of land. Look at all the land this motorway has taken up!

Cars are also a basic part of modern life. Everyone wants one and the car industry employs thousands of people. The economy of a country like Britain depends on it. But does this have to be the result?

Questions

You are interviewing an architect now. Find out:

1 if there was a clear difference between town and country 100 years ago
2 what has changed all that
3 what motorways do to the countryside
4 if motorways take up very much land
5 in what way cars are a basic part of modern life

4

But industry and modern life do not have to be enemies of beauty. This is a picture of a modern power station in Scotland. It proves that progress needn't be ugly. It doesn't have to destroy all the countryside around it. We can have beauty and progress if we really want to. We need clean rivers and open countryside just as much as people did 100 years ago. Perhaps, in some ways, we need them even more. Things like open land, clean water and good air are getting scarcer and scarcer.

Questions

Continue the interview with the architect. Find out:

1 if industry and modern life have to be enemies of beauty
2 what the thing in this picture is
3 if it proves anything
4 if we really need clean rivers and open countryside
5 what is getting scarcer and scarcer

5

Discussion

Imagine a discussion between two men. One thinks that a new factory ought to be built in a huge forest. It will produce a lot of smoke, dirt and filth, but also jobs in a place where there is a lot of unemployment. The other thinks the forest and the clean river are more important than economic advantages. What reasons would each give for his point of view?

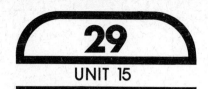

UNIT 15

We have made progress in *industry* and *science.*

1a

Comment

We do not use *the, a* or *an* with nouns like these when they indicate the thing *in general, the idea* of the thing *rather than a particular example of it.* For example:

> **I'm studying** *science.* (the thing in general)
> **Physics is** *an* **exact** *science.* (a particular example)

1b

Guided invention exercise

Now think of examples of such words used for the thing in general. For example, respond as B does.

> A: **I'd like to be a scientist.**
> B: **Then you ought to study science!**

1 I want to be an artist.
2 I'd like to be a mathematician.
3 What do I have to do if I want to be a doctor?
4 And what if I want to be an economist?
5 What do engineers study?
6 And chemists?
7 What about architects?
8 And musicians?
9 And what's that subject called that deals with Shakespeare, Dante, Goethe, Hemingway, Molière, etc?

1c

Now look through texts 1, 2, 3 and 4 again. Find all the examples you can of words used to indicate the thing in general or its idea.

1d

Now study this conversation. Two friends, A and B, are talking about their likes and dislikes. Notice that B does not use *the* even when he adds an adjective here.

> A: **I like wine . . . but it must be French!**
> B: **In other words, you like French wine.**

Now respond as B did.

1 I like jazz . . . particularly the old-fashioned type.
2 I like food . . . but not if it's English.
3 I enjoy music . . . especially the classical type.
4 I want to learn something about grammar. You see, I'm learning English.
5 Sport is interesting . . . particularly if it's cruel and blood-thirsty.
6 I don't like architecture . . . I mean this modern sort!
7 I'm fond of antiques . . . especially these old English ones.

1e

Comment

The is not used here because B is still thinking in general terms. There is no particular example that is referred to.

1f

Transfer

Imagine you are listing the subjects that can be studied at a very large adult education centre. Choose the main subjects from column A. Then add appropriate adjectives from column B.

A

architecture, music, jazz, literature, industry, art, science, physics, chemistry, mathematics, engineering, cooking, history, literature, drawing, book-keeping, management, baby-care, hypnotism, speaking, flower-arrangement, philosophy, psychology, religion

B

classical, modern English, atomic, American, Negro, organic, inorganic, metal, French, nineteenth-century baroque, vegetarian, commercial, radio, television, nude, public and after-dinner, machine, Japanese, oriental, twentieth-century, ancient

 **Modern industry
The car industry**

2a

Comment

The car industry is a specific example of a specific industry; the product is actually defined. That is why *the* is used. *Modern industry*, however, is still a general category. It is not a specific industry at all.

2b

Now make sentences, sometimes adding *the*, sometimes omitting it.

Model A

> **I want a job in industry.**
> **heavy: I want a job in heavy industry.**
> **car: I want a job in the car industry.**

I want a job in industry.

1 British
2 American
3 furniture
4 toy
5 modern
6 machine
7 clothes
8 textile
9 German

Model B

> **Life is full of surprises.**
> **city: City life is full of surprises.**
> **of a doctor: The life of a doctor is full of surprises.**

Life is full of surprises.

1 of a young child
2 modern
3 of a housewife
4 twentieth-century
5 of a salesman
6 City
7 Country
8 of a teacher

2c

Transfer

You are going to give a lecture at the adult education centre.
Your subject is: Noise in general.
You say: "This evening I'm going to talk about noise."
You are also going to talk about: the type of noise made by low-flying planes.
You say: "I'm also going to talk about the noise made by low-flying planes."

Now make two such statements about each of these topics.

1 health (in general and that of old people)
2 industry (in general and that of this town)
3 progress (in general and that made in the last century)

Noise and pollution

Two people are interviewed about the problems of noise and pollution. One is a young student. She lives near a large airport outside London. The second is an architect.

1

Vocabulary

dreadful: terrible, awful.

politicians: people engaged professionally in politics.

MP: abbreviation for "Member of Parliament": the person in Parliament who represents a particular area.

pollution: industrial filth, waste, noise, etc., that destroy or pollute peace, quiet and natural beauty.

sewers: underground canals, pipes, etc., used for removing waste and filth.

minor: (here) very small, unimportant.

thunder by: (here) used as verb with the meaning of "make a dreadful noise".

intolerable noise: noise it is impossible to put up with or live with.

2

Questions (to be answered after you have heard the tape)

2a

About the student who lives near the airport

1 What was the area like when she went to school?
2 What does she say about the noise now?
3 Why is it so much noisier now?
4 What have she and other people done about the noise?
5 Why does she think nothing has happened?

2b

The young architect

1 What, according to him, will happen if we don't deal with pollution?
2 What do we do to our rivers and lakes?
3 Why does he think we must clean up our rivers and lakes?
4 When the architect says, "That's only a minor example", does he mean:
   (a) it doesn't really matter if we don't clean them up
   (b) far worse things will happen if we don't
5 He says noise is a problem even though some get used to it. Why?
6 What are some of the effects of noise which he describes?
7 What does he say about "the whole planet"?
8 The interviewer asks if we can afford to deal with the problem; what is the architect's answer?

3

Summary

Use these short notes to summarise the interview.

1 the student/near an airport
2 to school and/up there
3 much quieter but now/worse and worse
4 planes/lower; traffic/heavier
5 up to London last month/MP
6 absolutely nothing because/live with the noise
7 architect thinks/deal with/or/planet any longer
8 if we go on/pollute/rivers and lakes/drinking water/few years' time
9 a lot of people/sleep properly/lorries/night after night
10 windows/hot nights
11 millions of people/intolerable noise
12 whole planet/murdered
13 something/done/very soon

4

Discussion (and/or extended writing)

1 Do you know a lake, river or place that used to be quiet but which has now been "polluted" by noise or dirt? Describe it.
2 What exactly do you think the architect means when he says, "Can we afford not to?" How would you answer the question? Give reasons.

Linda becomes very pessimistic about the future.

1

Story

Life was beginning to get Linda down. London sometimes seemed intolerably noisy and dirty. At times she felt very lonely. But now there was something worse. There were rumours going about that the EBC was in financial trouble, and would have to cut down on staff. Linda knew that since she had been one of the last to come, she would probably be one of the first to go. Then, one Friday afternoon, she was told that Wilson wanted to see her. Her heart sank. People always got the sack just before the weekend.

Wilson looked uncomfortable. He said he had meant to tell her something earlier but had forgotten. Linda almost broke down. She went very pale. She could feel her heart thumping. Wilson asked her if she was all right. She bore up somehow and asked him to go on. Then he said that the department had certain difficulties and that he would like to explain them to her. She sat back and waited for the blow to come.

"We're expanding the department; taking on new staff. But there's a shortage of space. I wonder if you'd mind sharing your office with two new reporters. It's only temporary," he said. Linda was so relieved she hardly knew what to say. Then Wilson mentioned that he would like to put her in charge of training the new reporters. "There'll be a rise for you, of course," he added.

2

Vocabulary

Find the words or phrases that mean:

1 depress her
2 reports, stories that may or may not be true
3 reduce the number of jobs
4 intended to
5 collapse in tears
6 go white
7 beat loudly
8 not collapse
9 very little room
10 use with others
11 make larger
12 employ more people
13 will last for only a short time
14 much better; less afraid
15 responsible for

3

Questions

1 Which things were getting Linda down?
2 Describe the rumours.
3 Why did she think she would get the sack?
4 Why did her heart sink that Friday?
5 How did the interview begin?
6 Describe Linda's feelings.
7 What exactly was it that Wilson said that made ·her feel relieved?

 Practice

4a

■ She had been one of the *last to come.*

In the same way say that she did these things among the last. She:

1 started work
2 heard the rumours
3 went out to lunch
4 was told about it
5 was given a rise
6 saw Wilson that day

4b

Transfer

You are writing an essay on "Pioneers in Science, Art and Technology". List some of the *people* or *countries* who *were the first to do* certain things.

4c

■ She waited for *the blow to come.*

What did she wait for if she thought that:

1 he would give her the sack
2 her heart would stop thumping
3 the phone would ring
4 the weather would clear up

4d

Transfer

You went to the Olympic Games. Describe the excitement and expectation in phrases like, "The crowd sat there, waiting for a new world record to be made." For example, say what happened before:

1 the gates opened
2 the flame was lit
3 the 100 metre race began

Dialogue/Practice

Listen. Then take Wilson's part.

Practice

1

Dialogue

WILSON: .... something .... tell you. I mean, I .... tell .... forgot.

LINDA: Yes. I see.

WILSON: .... your position. .... department.

LINDA: Oh. I see.

WILSON (*noticing she is pale*): .... all right?

LINDA: Yes. Please go on.

WILSON: Well, you see, the department .... difficulties. I'd .... explain .... you. Uh, by ...., how long .... working for us now?

LINDA: Almost a year exactly.

WILSON: Yes, ... certain changes .... make now.

LINDA: Changes? In the staff you mean?

WILSON: .... partly. You see, ... expanding ....

LINDA: Expanding it?

WILSON: Yes. That ...., ... more staff.

LINDA: I see. So those are the changes!

WILSON: .... shortage .... space.

LINDA: Not enough offices, you mean?

WILSON: Exactly. And .... ask you if (*pauses*) ....

LINDA: Yes. Go on.

WILSON: If .... mind .... your office .... two new .... It's only ....

LINDA: Sharing my office? No. Of course not.

WILSON: .... like .... you. I mean, I should like .... avoided it, but .... help it. There .... space.

LINDA: No, it's quite all right. I understand. Really.

WILSON: And then .... else.

LINDA: Something else?

WILSON: Yes, ... reporters. I .... you .... charge .... training.

LINDA: In charge of their training? Me?

WILSON: Yes. Do .... it on? The .... job, ...

LINDA: Yes. I'd be glad to.

WILSON: The new reporters .... next week. Oh, ... way, ... rise .... you, ... An .... £15 ....

LINDA: That makes it even better, doesn't it?

WILSON: Yes. Well, ... glad .... out of the way.

LINDA: Yes. So am I!

2a

▎ **"I was going to tell you but I forgot."**

You are Wilson. In the same way, tell Linda that you didn't:

1 speak to her about it; you were too busy
2 phone her; her line was engaged
3 give her a rise last month; the Financial Controller stopped you
4 see her this morning; you had to leave the office
5 discuss it with her; you had no time

2b

Transfer

Use this pattern to make typical excuses for not:

1 writing to someone
2 visiting someone
3 doing some homework
4 paying back some money
5 buying a friend a birthday present

2c

▎ **"I'd like to have avoided it."**

In the same way say you wanted to do these things but were unable to:

1 see that film
2 buy a better present
3 be at the last Olympic Games
4 come to the party
5 go to the dance

2d

Transfer

A few weeks ago you went to a famous city on business. You had very little time and were very busy. Now you are talking about all the things you'd like to have done there. What are they?

Grammar Summary/Revision

PHRASAL VERBS
(Type 4)

1a This is the simplest type of all. These verbs are used intransitively and consist of:

	verb	particle
She	broke	down
She	bore	up

These and other common ones, many of which you have already learned, appear in the short newspaper article below.

FIRE BREAKS OUT IN HOUSE – FLAMES DIE OUT BEFORE FIRE ENGINE PULLS UP
A small fire broke out in the home of Mrs Patricia Evans, 17 Merrow Avenue, yesterday. It all started when a small pan of milk boiled over. Mrs Evans pulled the pan away from the stove but her apron suddenly went up in smoke. She threw the apron down next to a tin of cleaning fluid. The cleaning fluid blew up. Luckily it was a very small explosion. Mrs Evans immediately rang up the local fire brigade, who dashed off immediately. However, half way there, the engine broke down. The men managed to repair it and started up again. Then, however, the petrol ran out. By the time the engine drew up outside Mrs Evans' house, the flames had died out. Unfortunately the house had also burnt down.

Questions **1b**
1 Describe how the fire started.
2 Describe what happened after Mrs Evans rang the fire brigade up.

■ **The new reporters start next week.**

PRESENT SIMPLE
(Future use)

2 The present simple can be used to describe things in the future that are *part of a set plan*. Make examples yourself describing:

1 the schedule for the next Olympic Games
2 a railway timetable
3 a bank robbery planned for tomorrow and worked out with military precision by four ex-officers
4 what a secretary would tell her boss about his timetable for tomorrow.

EXTENDED WRITING
(and/or oral practice)

3 Write either a short story or a dialogue based on these facts.

A young man, Arthur Howe, works in a travel agency in London. He is feeling very depressed. He has heard that the agency is going to close down. Then, at the end of the month, he is told the head of the agency (call him Mr Morgan) wants to see him.

At the beginning Morgan says several things that make Arthur believe he is going to lose his job. But Morgan really only wants to ask him to take his holidays later than planned. They are opening a new office in Manchester. He offers Arthur the post of manager of the new office.

ACKNOWLEDGEMENTS

We are grateful to the following for permission to reproduce copyright material:

Barnaby's Picture Library for page 121 top; Camera Press for pages 24 top photo by Pickerell, 33 top photo by Colin Davey, 40 top left photo by Gerry Granham, 81 photo by Mark Yate, 120 bottom; J. Allan Cash for page 112 bottom; CEDO for pages 8 bottom, 16 bottom; Fox Photos for pages 8 centre, 72; Illustrated Newspapers Ltd for page 56; International Language Centre for page 32 bottom; Keystone Press Agency for page 8 top; London Express News & Feature Services for page 65; The Mansell Collection for pages 57 top, 80 top; James Marsh for page 73 top; Oxfam for pages 40 top right, 40 bottom; Paul Popper for pages 25 bottom, 41, 57 bottom; Press Association for pages 80 bottom, 112 top; Presse-Illustrations-Bureau for page 73 bottom; Servizio Informazioni, Rome for page 32 top; Trustees of The London Museum for page 120 top; United Kingdom Atomic Energy Authority for page 121 bottom; United States Information Service for page 25 top.

We are grateful to the following artists for:

Edward McLachlan for pages 48, 49, 88, 89, 97; Jim Russell (Saxon Artists) for pages 16 top, 33 bottom, 96, 105.

LONGMAN GROUP LIMITED
London

Associated companies, branches and representatives throughout the world

© Eurozentren 1973

First published 1973
Fifth impression 1975

ISBN 0 582 52242 0

Filmset by Keyspools Ltd, Golborne, Lancs

Printed in Great Britain by Lowe & Brydone (Printers) Ltd, Thetford, Norfolk